"*Dwell Differently* is an invitation we all need—to know, love, and apply God's Word to our everyday lives. No matter who you are or where you are in your journey with Christ, this book is sure to encourage your heart, mind, and soul."

Ruth Chou Simons, *Wall Street Journal* bestselling author,
artist, and founder of GraceLaced.com

"Living in a biblically illiterate generation is scary, because then we as imperfect, broken humans get to pick what truth becomes. I'm really grateful that Natalie and Vera have decided to press into the joy and life-changing practice of learning and clinging to God's truth. This book grips the reality that when our imperfect, broken world has no answers, God's truth has them all. That's real good news."

Toni Collier, speaker, podcaster, and author of
Brave Enough to Be Broken

"Dwell has been helping people memorize Scripture for years, and now this resource is full of reminders of why it matters. There is power in the words of the Bible, and by the end of this book, I am confident you'll be a different person."

Jamie Ivey, author and host of the podcast
The Happy Hour with Jamie Ivey

"Gospel-rich and accessible to every kind of reader, *Dwell Differently* celebrates the goodness of God's Word and shows you how to apply it to real-life circumstances. With warmth and transparency, Vera and Natalie will turn your eyes again and again toward the Savior who loves you so."

Glenna Marshall, author of *The Promise Is His Presence*,
Everyday Faithfulness, and *Memorizing Scripture*

"Vera and Natalie's words feel like wise counsel from a kind friend. I will eagerly commend this book to my own teen daughters and my friends who are new to following Jesus. But it's not only for the young or the young in faith. Those who have walked with Christ for decades will also be deeply encouraged by this book and the timeless practice of abiding in God's Word. No Christian is ever too young or too old to dwell differently in God's truth."

Jen Oshman, author, podcaster, women's ministry director

dwell

DIFFERENTLY

dwell
DIFFERENTLY

**OVERCOME NEGATIVE THINKING WITH THE
SIMPLE PRACTICE OF MEMORIZING GOD'S TRUTH**

Natalie Abbott and Vera Schmitz

DESIGNS BY VERA SCHMITZ

BETHANYHOUSE

a division of Baker Publishing Group
Minneapolis, Minnesota

© 2024 by Dwell Differently, LLC

Published by Bethany House Publishers
Minneapolis, Minnesota
BethanyHouse.com

Bethany House Publishers is a division of
Baker Publishing Group, Grand Rapids, Michigan

Printed in China

Library of Congress Cataloging-in-Publication Data
Names: Abbott, Natalie, author. | Schmitz, Vera Margarita, author.
Title: Dwell differently : overcome negative thinking with the simple practice of memorizing God's truth / Natalie Abbott and Vera Schmitz.
Description: Minneapolis, Minnesota : Bethany House Publishers, a division of Baker Publishing Group, [2024] | Includes bibliographical references.
Identifiers: LCCN 2023039779 | ISBN 9780764242540 (cloth) | ISBN 9781493446742 (ebook)
Subjects: LCSH: Bible—Memorizing. | Bible—Study and teaching.
Classification: LCC BS617.7 .A23 2024 | DDC 248.8/6—dc23/eng/20231019
LC record available at https://lccn.loc.gov/2023039779

The proprietor is represented by Alive Literary Agency, AliveLiterary.com.

Designs and cover by Vera Schmitz

Interior design by Nadine Rewa

Baker Publishing Group publications use paper produced from sustainable forestry practices and post-consumer waste whenever possible.

24   25   26   27   28   29   30   7   6   5   4   3   2   1

For Jason, Josiah, Esther, Mimi, Ezra, and Silas
—Natalie

For my boys
—Vera

Contents

DEAR FRIEND,

Okay, maybe not friend yet . . . but soon, by the end of this book, we hope you'll feel like a friend—like someone who knows us (really, really). We're sisters who love each other and Jesus . . . and warm buttery tortillas and late-night laughter and swapping clothes and all the things that make us sisters. We're also co-founders of Dwell Differently, a ministry and podcast that helps thousands of women find true life change through the simple practice of memorizing God's truth. Now we're bringing Dwell Differently to you in this book. We are completely ecstatic!

And we want to invite you in.

Yes, we're inviting you in to the Dwell method. But more than that, we're inviting you in to our lives—not just our sunny-day, post-worthy parts, but the uncurated, uncut versions of our lives—to show you the profound impact of dwelling in God's truth. We have seen victory and joy and goodness sprout up where there was only fear and insecurity and struggle. And this is what we want for you.

We want to help you overcome your negative thoughts with God's truth.

In this book, we're going to equip you to do just that. We're going to help you memorize eleven Bible verses (in a shockingly simple way!). We're going to teach you what they mean, tell you why they matter, show you how they've helped us overcome our struggles, and prompt you to consider how they might help you too. This is our hope and our prayer and our joy: to give you God's own true words so you can overcome your negative thoughts. We pray that victory and joy and goodness will sprout up from God's words planted in your heart and mind as you grow in love and knowledge of him.

Warmly and sincerely,
Vera & Natalie

YOU NEED
TRUTH

1

How Are You Doing, *Really?*

VERA

"Everyone Has Stuff"

A few weeks ago, my husband, Matt, and I got together with four other couples for dinner. We do this friendship dinner once a month, where we share a meal and the hosts of the meal ask one question. While we sit together, we all answer the question. It might be a prompt that helps us know something about each person's childhood, or who impacted them the most in their high school years, or what life lesson they hope most to teach their children. It's a beautiful meal full of intentionality, laughter, and the joy of community. Two Sundays ago, the question was simple: "How are you?" There was one caveat: you were not allowed to answer with the words *fine* or *good*. What transpired over the next hour and a half was raw and real and a very clear reminder—we all have stuff. Big stuff. Work stuff. Health stuff. Relationship (marriage, friend, children) stuff. Past stuff. Present stuff. Just stuff. When we left that night, Matt looked at me and said something he says a lot: "I forget it sometimes, but we are *all* walking around with stuff. All of us."

What about You?

I want to ask you, *How are you?* Like really, *really*. How are you doing? My guess is that you aren't good or fine. Whether your pain point or problem is right at the surface or it's something that you try to bury deep in you, it's there. If you answered honestly, you might tell me that your current circumstances are completely overwhelming you, and your spirit feels crushed beneath the weight of it all. Maybe the unknown of life scares you to death, and you just wish you knew what to do next. Maybe you're anxious all the time, and you feel like your negative thoughts hold you captive in your own mind. Maybe things are 98 percent great, but there's that last 2 percent lurking around the dark edges of your mind that, if you're honest, you have no idea what to do with. Like Matt said, "We all have stuff." But what do we do with it? And you may be thinking, *I've never had much success dealing with my stuff. What are you going to give me that's going to help?*

If I Could Give You *One Thing*

If I could know your answer to *How are you?*, if I knew your intimate secrets and the deepest longings of your heart, if I knew your greatest struggle, if I could see all the negative things you tell yourself, if I could look you straight in the eye and give you just *one thing*, I would give you God's Word.

God's Word leading you
God's Word healing your broken places
God's Word fighting the lies
God's Word encouraging your heart
God's Word battling your insecurities
God's Word giving you purpose
God's Word in the middle of the night
God's Word all day long

God's Word for life and blessing and joy
God's Word helping you overcome negative thoughts
God's Word for you

No matter if you were my best friend, my worst enemy, the president, or my kid, if I had the privilege of knowing you and your struggle, God's Word is the one thing I would labor to give to you. Why? Just one verse, one small word from God is more powerful, more impactful, more beautiful, and more grounding than any other thing I could give you.

Why Is God's Word the Thing?

In his Word, the Bible, the God of everything big, small, vast, and deep is telling you his story, a story he wants to invite you into, a story about his goodness and his good plan to make all things right. God's words aren't just a self-help strategy, they are our best and only hope. His words are powerful because he is powerful. His words are beautiful because he is beautiful. God's words ground us because in them we find every true thing, every answer we need—not just to overcome our negative thoughts, but why we have them at all—what's wrong with the world, and how we can find hope and joy and goodness. All his promises are in that book, and they are true for any and all who would believe them. They are so, so, so good. The words we are going to learn are God's words.

God Has Something to Say to You Specifically

My fingers are flying across this keyboard right now because I am so amped up to share this with you! I want to hop on my chair and throw my arms wide and proclaim at the top of my lungs that God has something to say to you! God has something to say specifically, individually, right now, and each and every day to *you*. He wants to step into your life, your every moment, your problems, your joys, your projects, and your purpose through his Word. And his words for your life—those words aren't just true and helpful, they are the actual voice of God speaking into your life, even now. No matter your circumstances, God has a relevant, powerful word for you. And even just one verse has the power to change everything.

How Just One Verse Changed Me

I know the power of just one verse, because I've seen it again and again in my own life. God used just one verse to reach into my fear at eight years old and change my heart and my eternity (Matthew 17:20). God used just one verse to fuel me to run after him in high school when so many of my friends were going the opposite direction (John 10:10). God used just one verse to comfort and care for my soul when I was in the darkest season of my life (Romans 8:15). I want to give you God's Word because through it, God has truly changed my life. It is bread for my soul, a light on my path, and the hope for every struggle or situation I encounter. When you stand on one verse, when you fix your mind on it, when you speak it to your heart until it takes root, it changes everything. And because God has changed me through the power of his Word, I've made it my life mission to give people that one thing. I help people memorize Bible verses.

I know how that sounds. Super churchy. But what if God's Word really is *the thing*? What if putting it in your head and heart changes everything? What if it's exactly what you need? And here I am, up here on a chair again, trying to convince you:

God's. Word. Is. The. Thing.

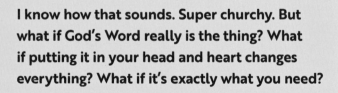

I know how that sounds. Super churchy. But what if God's Word really is the thing? What if putting it in your head and heart changes everything? What if it's exactly what you need?

I believe this so strongly that I've committed my life to helping people memorize Scripture. After God rescued me out of the absolute darkest season of my life with his true words, I just had to help other people too. So my sister Natalie and I started a ministry called Dwell Differently. We have a ridiculously simple method of memorizing Bible verses (and you're going to learn it in this book!). And what started with a handful of friends and family has turned into thousands of people memorizing and meditating on one Bible verse every month. We send out monthly verse memory kits, host a weekly podcast, post weekly devotions, and show up on all the socials. Seriously. We are over here doing every possible thing we can think of to help people get God's Word into their hearts and minds for real life change.

Here's Where You Come In

We wrote this book to give even more people (i.e., you!) *the thing*, God's Word in your head and heart. In it we're going to learn and lean into eleven verses that speak a better word than the negative things we tend to say to ourselves. We are going to help you replace the lies and the doubts and the wrong thoughts in your mind with God's true words. And I can't tell you how pumped I am to learn these verses along with you! I just know that God is going to do extraordinary things through the seemingly ordinary practice of memorizing his words. *I can't wait to get started!*

Where We're Going: The Roadmap

Before we get going, I want to tell you where we're headed and how we're going to get there. We're headed to victory over our negative thinking! Can you imagine?! And let me tell you how we're going to get there: we're in this *together*. Natalie and I aren't just here to give you some helpful tools or a great how-to formula. No, we're actually going to walk through each negative thought pattern with you first, showing how we've struggled in each area. Then we're going to see what God has to say about it in his Word. And finally, we're going to help you interact with God in his Word through questions, prayers, prompts, and the like. So, each chapter will have three main components: our problem, the solution, and your interaction.

1. Our Problem: Negative Thoughts

In each chapter of this book, either Natalie or I will address a particular negative thought pattern. These are things we've struggled with too! So, we'll give you examples from our own lives. But the goal isn't merely to be relatable—it's also to get your mind working on how you may struggle in the same area. Often, we have trouble identifying our negative thought patterns. So, we'll give you examples of what those sneaky negative thoughts sound like when they creep into our heads. We're going to model for you how we've personally identified and battled our negative thoughts with God's truth.

Want to hear more? Natalie and I made a limited podcast series just for this book. Each verse has its own episode, where we talk honestly about what we've learned and how God has met us in it. Here's a QR code for that. You'll see that code throughout the book wherever we want to take you to all that extra good stuff!

2. The Solution: God's TRUTH

This is it! This is the *one thing* I was talking about—God's own words to help you overcome your negative thoughts! But we aren't just going to help you put these words in your head like some magic spell to say over yourself to ward off bad thoughts. No, these verses are so much more than a mantra: these are the very words of God, who is all wise, all loving, and all good. They are deep and true and powerful. So, we're going to dive into each verse, learning the meaning behind what we're memorizing. We want you to see where each verse fits into God's love song for his people, what it means, and why it matters. Only then can we rightly apply it to our own lives.

But we aren't just going to help you put these words in your head like some magic spell to say over yourself to ward off bad thoughts. No, these verses are so much more than a mantra: these are the very words of God, who is all wise, all loving, and all good.

In each chapter, we're going to memorize a specific verse that fights each negative thought pattern. We chose eleven verses. I know, eleven verses might sound overwhelming. But we've made it super simple. We've created eleven unique verse designs to help you memorize each verse and help them stick in your mind long-term. I'll show you how it works in the next chapter. Moreover, we've made all the things to help you memorize these verses: free screen-savers, downloadable coloring sheets, and you can even purchase temporary tattoos (so you can memorize your verses on the go!).

One last note here: you can skip ahead! If you're dealing with something really hard, by all means, go to that chapter first. Each chapter is a stand-alone look at one particular struggle, somewhat like a reference book. You'll want to finish out this chapter and read the next one so you can learn how the memory method works, but once you've done that, feel free to flip back to the table of contents and go where you need to go!

3. Your Interaction: Apply the TRUTH

Friend, if this book is anything, it is *for you*. It's for your good, for your help, for your personal life change. It's not for merely drilling verses into your head. Who cares if you learn every verse in the Bible, but they don't actually seep way down deep into your heart and transform you? God commands his people not just to fix his words in their minds but also their hearts (Deuteronomy 11:18). And we want you to do just that—to let God's words find a place in your heart for real life change. Sooooo, interact with this book, write in it, underline it, highlight it! Heck, tear out a page and tape it to your bathroom mirror to remind yourself what God says about who he is and who you are every time you look at yourself. This book is all yours. Use it as you see fit!

One last thing. Get a journal or a blank notebook. At the end of every chapter, we're going to be asking you questions in a section called "Apply the TRUTH." These are questions we want you to wrestle with and answer. We're going to give you prompts to prod you into deeper thinking and challenge you to pray and seek God in your struggles. You're going to want a place to write down your answers, thoughts, and prayers. And you'll want a place to practice writing out your memory verses. Even if you aren't a journaler, you probably are going to want a designated processing space. And if you write down what you're learning, you'll be able to look back and see all that God has done for you through the simple practice of memorizing and meditating on his true words.

Apply the TRUTH

This is the place for you to consider what we've discussed in the chapter and apply it to your life. In this chapter, we talked about how we all have stuff. But the real question for you (and me) is, "How are you going to deal with it?" I've put together a few questions to help you start thinking about what you want to get out

Get the Companion Resources!

Listen to the *Dwell Differently* book podcast

- Listen while you read! In each episode, Natalie and Vera will discuss a chapter of the book. They'll chat about what they're learning from the verses, their victories, and their struggles to overcome negative thinking with God's truth.

Get free digital downloads of the verse designs

- Phone, watch, and computer lock screens
- Coloring sheets

Purchase the *Dwell Differently* companion items

- Items like temporary tattoos to help you easily memorize each verse
- The *Dwell Differently Journal*

Go to: DwellDifferently.com/OvercomeNegativeThinking

of this book. (Here's the part where you are going to want to get out that journal!) I've just told you my hopes for you, but what are *your* hopes for you? Specifically. Take some time to reflect and pray through these questions:

- Was there ever a time when you really clung to a Bible verse or one of God's promises? What specifically about that verse spoke to you and your situation?
- How are you doing, *really*? What are some of the things you're struggling with right now?

- What are your fears or reservations about confronting those struggles?
- What are your hopes for memorizing God's truth?
- Look through the table of contents. Which chapter are you most anxious to read? Why?
- Here's a prayer for you as you start out on this journey:

God,

Would you meet me here? Would you help me be honest and vulnerable, so I can see my true self and all of my stuff? You already know it all, and you want better for me. Here are some of the negative thoughts I struggle with:

Will you help me memorize and meditate on your words so that I can find freedom and joy? Help me really understand and believe in your true words. They are powerful because they are from you. Please use them to work change in my heart and actions. Specifically, these are my hopes:

They are the deep things of my heart and things only you can give. I trust you with them. And I pray with expectancy, knowing that you see me, you hear me, and you love me. O God, do what you alone can do in my life.

Amen

What God's Word Says about God's Word

Ever wonder what the Bible says about itself? Psalm 119 is a great place to go to read about the power of God's Word in the lives of those who believe it. Here are a few of the things listed there.

God's Word

Exposes my wrong thoughts, motivations, and actions
Elevates me when I'm low
Humbles me when I'm prideful
Makes the simple person (me) wise
Lights my path
Blesses me
Keeps me from shame
Keeps my way pure
Keeps me from sinning against God
Brings me great delight
Gives me life
Overflows in me
Cuts through the lies
Defends me
Strengthens me
Encourages me
Brings me joy and contentment
Gives me life
Confirms God's promises to his people
Gives me an answer when there is none
Gives me hope
Comforts me in my hardships

A
GOOD
MAN
BRINGS
GOOD
THINGS
OUT
OF THE
GOOD
STORED
UP IN HIS
HEART.
LUKE 6:45A

agmbgt
oOtgSu
ihh

L6·45A

2

TRUTH to Overcome NEGATIVE THINKING

VERA

A good man brings good things out of the good stored up in his heart.

—Luke 6:45a

What's Going On in Our Heads?

We have only begun to scratch the surface of understanding the human brain. But what we *do* know about our thought life is pretty astounding. Studies differ on how many thoughts we have in a day, but it's probably more than you think. A recent study estimates that we have over 6,000 thoughts a day,[1] and naturally many of those thoughts are repetitive. But here's the stark and startling reality about all those thousands of repetitive thoughts streaming through our heads: most studies conclude that the majority of those thoughts are negative. One such study concludes that humans are naturally wired to think negatively as a means of avoiding future harm.[2] So, we have thousands of thoughts speeding through our minds all day long, and most of them are negative thoughts on a repetitive soundtrack. Yikes!

The first time I read about this, I was shocked. Sure, I knew I had negative thoughts, but I had no idea that *most* of my thoughts were probably negative, and that I was living a sort of Groundhog Day of the same negative thoughts over and over again. That's a lot! And those negative thoughts on repeat, all day every day, are creating pathways in my brain. Every time I think a thought, I am likely to come back and think it again. And that repetitive way of thinking forms pathways in our brain. The more we travel them, the deeper the ruts get in the road. Or to think of it another way, what started out as a small path becomes a paved road and eventually turns into a seven-lane highway. It felt overwhelming to know this and daunting to imagine how I might make a change! Would it be possible to experience anything different? Or would I forever be subject to the worn-out pathways of negative thinking in my head?

There Is a Different Path

I can tell you from experience (not just mine, but from so many others), there is help. Yes and *amen*! There is a solution. You *can* form new paths of thinking. You can create new, good thought pathways. And thankfully, you are holding this book, which offers a proven, biblical method for getting off the negative superhighways in your brain and forming new good and true pathways of thinking. We are going to teach you how to replace the lies and the doubts and the wrong thoughts in your mind with God's true words.

Now, I'm going to make a leap here and assume that if you are reading this book, you believe or at least are considering believing that the Bible is true. Perfect! What I love about the Bible is that you don't have to have your ducks in a row in order to interact with it—it will unfold and bring life and light to anyone who seeks God in it. So wherever you are, you're welcome here, even if you are feeling skeptical.

What I love about the Bible is that you don't have to have your ducks in a row in order to interact with it—it will unfold and bring life and light to anyone who seeks God in it.

The Paths We're On: Negative Superhighways

Before we can get started on the good paths we want to travel, we need to take a peek into our own heads and see the negative superhighways we're traveling day in and day out. One common one is the feeling that we are unlovable. These thoughts tell us we aren't pretty enough or smart enough or valuable enough to be loved. Or maybe one of our superhighways is that we're unacceptable. These thoughts center around all the ways we fail to measure up, all the things we didn't do, and all the ways we've not succeeded. Another possible superhighway is fear. These are all our worst-case-scenario thoughts, the things that we Google and shouldn't, and all the bad possibilities that come at us time and time again. I've just mentioned a few things here, but do you see the pattern? Do you have patterns like this too? What are the superhighways of negativity you're traveling?

You Can Get on a Better Path

What if we could reroute and start down some new walking paths of truth in our mind? At first, they will be just that—little, tiny walking paths—but those walking paths will begin to wear in and become country lanes, then major four-lane roads, and eventually superhighways of truth in our minds. What if this were possible? If it's possible for the bad, then it must also be possible for the good!

God's Word, a Better Path

In this book, we plan to fix our minds on what God says is true and beautiful and good. And we have the easiest way to help you dwell in it, meditate on it, and speak it to yourself until you have a superhighway in your brain filled with God's Word—truth about who he is, how he loves you, how he gives you power over sin, how he equips you to fight anxiety and fear, how he is your one good thing in this world! His Word holds the true affirmations we will speak over ourselves and the thoughts

we will fix our minds on! These affirmations are where our peace and confidence will find their firm foundation.

Wait—is she talking about Bible verse memorization?

Why yes, yes I am. This might be something that you don't want to do, don't know how to do, don't believe you *can* do. But I'm going to challenge you for one moment to stop and really check in with yourself. If you look deep enough, way deep down, I'm gonna guess that if you really think about the freedom that is available to you, the idea of having God's true words about you—his loving, purpose-filled, safe, kind, generous words for your life—steeped in your brain and richly living in you, guiding your every thought, feeling, and action, you would admit that this is exactly what you want. You want a free mind and peace-filled spirit. Friend, these are available. It is possible. Even if you are skeptical, ask yourself, *If it really worked, wouldn't it be worth a try?* We're doing it one verse at a time, one chapter

at a time. We've picked eleven of the most common negative superhighways we humans find ourselves speeding down. We've
then prayerfully chosen a truth from God's Word to memorize
and say to ourselves, creating new good pathways in our mind.
Here are these pathways:

TRUTH to overcome NEGATIVE THINKING
TRUTH when you feel UNLOVED
TRUTH when you feel INSECURE
TRUTH when you feel UNACCEPTED
TRUTH when you're ANXIOUS
TRUTH when you're DEPRESSED
TRUTH when you're AFRAID
TRUTH when you need DIRECTION
TRUTH when you CAN'T PRAY
TRUTH when you need REST
TRUTH when you have TROUBLES

But memorizing is hard!
Okay, okay. Maybe. But here's where this book comes in. We've
made memorizing simple. It's going to be easier than learning
your state capitals (which I am actually not totally good on). I've
got just a few scientific reasons why the Dwell Differently method
is so simple and effective. Hang with me just a moment.

Many of us are visual learners. If you've ever tried to memorize
anything just by reading it or writing it out, you may have failed.
Either you didn't get it at all or you could only retain it long enough
to regurgitate it on a test, but then it was gone. I'm like you—not
a great memory for memorizing. But when information is put in
an image that relates to that information, it really does stick in
my head!

In writing this book, I actually stumbled upon a small experi-
ment done in a law class where the professor brought in art

painted by his wife that corresponded to each lesson. At the end of the semester, many of the students commented that the art had been very helpful, even indispensable in learning the course material.[3] The idea is that images help ideas burrow deep in our minds, carving out new spaces for new thoughts to make their way. Here's the point: when we have visual images to go along with what we're learning, we're far more successful in our recall of information. So for every verse you're going to memorize in this book, I've created a corresponding image to help you with your memorization.

The human brain is easily tricked. And we use that to our advantage. We put the first letter of every word of a verse into the corresponding design. When you see those letters, your mind is tricked into easily recalling the word itself. And this really helps you memorize the verse with ease.

Truth + Image = Memorization
Memorization + Meditation = New Thought Superhighways
New Thought Superhighways = Life Change

So, this is why we do what we do at Dwell Differently. We do it because we want to help your brain *dwell differently*. We want you to actually walk away from this book with God's words on repeat in your heart and mind (instead of those negative thoughts). That's our number-one goal here. So, we make it simple by using memory-prompting images and letters to make the verses stick. Let me show you how by teaching you a verse.

Good Input = Good Output

Let's dive right in. The basis of this book, the whole idea, is that when we memorize God's good truth, it helps us overcome our negative thinking. More than that, it *replaces* the bad thoughts with good ones. And when we have good thoughts in our minds, good things come out of us—things like peace and freedom and change in our thoughts and our actions. It seems then, that we should start with a verse about the promise that the Bible makes about how good things come out of us when we store up God's goodness in our hearts: "A good man brings good things out of the good stored up in his heart" (Luke 6:45a).

I love this verse! One, I love the simplicity, but two, I know people who live like this. I have experienced people who are truly content, joyful, and full of life and hope despite their circumstances. I've met these people and could say that they must have good in them because goodness just pours out of them. This is the true and real goodness that comes from knowing God and his Word. It certainly isn't pouring out of their hard situations! It's an otherworldly, baffling goodness, the kind of goodness Jesus promises in this verse. And I know this goodness is possible for my life because I have been the recipient of good things from men and women who have this goodness deep in them. What beauty! What we store up in our heart will pour out of our heart. And if we store up the good things of God in us, others will benefit from that goodness.

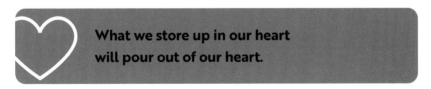

What we store up in our heart will pour out of our heart.

"A good man brings good things out of the good stored up in his heart" (Luke 6:45a). Yes. *Amen!* This is what I want to be said of me. Help me, Lord! The promise is this: when we store the good things of God in our heart (and in our mind), the outflow in our lives will be good things. And good things not only help us to be "good" and to live free and full, but they also impact those around us. It is a true and beautiful promise from the lips of Jesus himself, the kind of promise we should put in our heads.

Let's Get Memorizing!

Like our verse encourages us, let's store up these good words from God in our hearts. Let me show you how the Dwell Differently memory method works:

1. We start with our verse: "A good man brings good things out of the good stored up in his heart" (Luke 6:45a).
2. Then we take the first letter of each word in the verse, and we string them together in a long line of letters:

   A G M B G T O O T G S U I H H L6.45A
3. We take the letters and turn them into a beautiful Scripture design.

4. Every time you see the design, you're challenged to recall what each letter represents, and eventually you memorize the verse.

Boom! It really *is* that simple. When we are creating the design, we communicate the message of the verse through the image. So since this verse is about the heart, the image corresponds. Though the image is useful when you first commit the verse to memory, it also serves as a long-term memory prompt that's carved in your mind for later retrieval.

We want you to really fix that image in your mind. So, we've created lots of ways for you to see it all day long. We have a whole page of resources on our website devoted to each and every verse in this book. One resource we created is free lock screens for your phone and watch, so every time you glance at your phone or check the time, you're reminded of the verse (find the QR code for this at the end of this chapter). We want you to see that image everywhere you go so your mind is constantly prompted to recall the good, true words of God. And before you know it, you've memorized the verse!

This is it! This is what we're going to do in this book. We're going to fill your heart and mind with God's truth. We are going to help you dwell differently. So, when those negative thoughts come whispering in your ear, when anxiety threatens, when insecurity looms, you can talk back with truth. You can bring good things out of the good that you've stored up in your heart. You can fight the lies and negativity with the true and powerful Word of God.

Apply the TRUTH

- What are some of your negative superhighways?
- Pay attention to your thoughts as you go throughout your day. Keep track of whether they're mostly negative or positive. Are they repetitive? Come back and write some of them down. What surprised you? What were you already aware of?

- What good things do you desire for your thoughts?
- What good things do you desire for your emotions?
- What good things do you desire to see in your actions?
- Ask God for these things now. I might pray something like this: *Jesus, you promise good things for me when I store up good things in my heart. I know that you are my greatest good and that your Word helps me look more like you. Help me believe this is true and that you are at work in my life as I memorize and meditate on the good things you say. Lord, I want new pathways in my mind. Give me weapons of truth to fight my own thoughts and the lies of the enemy. And when I struggle to believe you have good things for me, please help me with my unbelief. Amen.*
- Download the digital verse design on your phone and practice saying it every time you pick up your phone.
- Find the podcast episode, lock screens, a coloring page, and temporary tattoos at DwellDifferently.com /OvercomeNegativeThinking.

A
GOOD
MAN
BRINGS
GOOD
THINGS
OUT
OF THE
GOOD
STORED
UP IN HIS
HEART.
LUKE 6:45A

agmbgt
oOtgSu
ihh
L6·45A

TRUTH

TO GROUND YOU

S
WG
LTFH
LOUTW
SBCCOG
ATIWWA♔

1J3.1A

SEE WHAT GREAT LOVE THE FATHER HAS LAVISHED ON US,
THAT WE SHOULD BE CALLED CHILDREN OF GOD!
AND THAT IS WHAT WE ARE!
I JOHN 3:1A

3

TRUTH When You Feel UNLOVED

NATALIE

See what great love the Father has lavished on us, that we should
be called children of God! And that is what we are!

—1 John 3:1a

You Are Loved

This is it. The one thing you need to hear and feel and understand.
You are loved. Period. All of you. As is. Right now. You are loved.

It's what every single human ever desperately needs to get—that
we are loved. We need our hearts filled with love like we need our
stomachs filled with food. But truth be told, when it comes to love,
most of us are starving. We go about our days filling ourselves up
with junk-food love—empty stuff that only leaves us hungrier than
ever for a real and lasting love that won't let us down, won't leave
us lonely and longing, singing along with so many sad love songs.

But is there really a love like that?

A love that can truly fill us? A love that won't abandon us—a
faithful love, a safe love, a love that's dependable and sure? Is
there a love out there that can carry us through life without letting
us down? Could there even be a love like that—the kind of love

we long for, the kind of love we deeply and desperately need?

Yes. There is. I know for sure.

I've experienced this love firsthand. It's a love that when my jaded and hurting heart first heard of it, I thought sounded absurd, fake, and too wonderful to be possible. And yet, when I finally reached out for it, I found it even more incredible than I could've imagined. It's a love so long you'll never come to the end of it, so patient you can never exasperate it, so sure you can build your life on it. It's a love I continue to discover and can't wait to discuss with you. It's the lavish love we were made for, a love that makes us its own. It's the love of God for us. *This* is the only love that can truly fill us and give us a firm foundation for our lives. And I am convinced that as we wrap ourselves up in this verse about God's extravagant love, it will not only reframe our thinking but will also work deep in our hearts to bring wholeness and healing.

This is the love you need, the love you so desperately want. This is the love of God for you. But maybe you don't feel very lovable, maybe you struggle to believe that you're worthy of God's love. It's a negative thought I often struggle with. *Why would anyone ever love me, let alone God, who's perfectly good and sees all of my deep dark secrets? How could he love me?* It's a negative thought that plagues us all at times, even on repeat, holding us captive, keeping us from experiencing the love that God has for us. In order to feel that love, we need to identify the negative thoughts that keep us from it.

Negative, Repetitive Loops

A couple of years ago, I was driving through a city I didn't know very well. I had the address in my phone, and the app was telling me where to go. It was a busy part of the city with several intersecting highways and a lot of cloverleaf exits. The app had me take one exit, which took me in a huge loop onto another highway. Then just as soon as I got on that highway, I was looped around onto another highway. Then, I was looped onto another. I was really starting to get turned around, literally. *Was I back on the original highway?* Thankfully, I noticed one of the billboards. I *was* back on the original highway. *What just happened?!* I ended up pulling off and looking back through my route. For some silly reason, my app had taken me in circles only to bring me back onto the same highway that I should've never left. I don't know if you've ever experienced a glitch like that on your navigational app, but it was pure ridiculousness! As much as we may not want to admit it, this is often what our brains do with our negative thoughts. We get ourselves into repetitive loops that we just can't seem to get out of, and some of them have to do with the essence of who we are.

The Loop We Get Stuck In: You Aren't Lovable

This is one of the most harmful negative loops we can get stuck in. It strikes at the very core of who we are—the place where we understand whether we are wanted and worthy of love. So, before we can dwell in the truth of God's love, we need to discover whether we can actually receive it or whether we're stuck in a negative loop that tells us his love isn't for us.

I Don't Believe That

Some of you might be thinking, *This isn't me.* But before you skip to the next chapter, I want to show you just how pernicious and sneaky this negative loop really is. When it comes to love, our thoughts often wander through a desert of lies—lies that tell us we're unlovable because of this or that flaw, lies that encourage us to posture, pose, and present ourselves in more lovable ways. And here's the staggering reality: most of the time we don't even recognize the lies we're believing. How are we going to exit the negative loop if we don't even recognize that we're stuck in it? It's a tricky task. You see, these negative loops often look like an oasis, masquerading as self-help or common sense or good advice.

So, I'm going to get real here and share some of my own negative, repetitive loops when it comes to love—these are the thoughts that work against me, telling me I'm unlovable, unwanted, and unworthy. I wonder if you can relate to some of them:

- *You should work harder at being the best version of yourself.*
- *You need to retake that picture, it looks terrible.*
- *You should be more friendly, outgoing, relatable, funny.*
- *If only you were more with it.*
- *If you were more like this or that, people would like you more.*
- *You sound stupid. Why did you say that?*
- *You don't need them anyway.*
- *You are way too much.*
- *You're not enough.*
- *You should be more like so-and-so.*
- *This is why people don't like you.*
- *No one would love you if they knew* that *about you.*
- *If they really loved you, they would act differently.*

Do any of these sound familiar to you?

I wonder what *your* negative thought loops are—the reasons *you* feel unlovable, unworthy, unwanted? At the end of this chapter, I'll encourage you to try to identify them. For now, though, I have a suspicion that I'm not alone here. And with thoughts like these playing on repeat in our heads, it's no wonder we doubt ourselves constantly and feel unloved and unlovable.

Our Negative Thoughts Lead to Actions

What is the fruit of thinking we're unlovable? We end up protecting ourselves by not being real or not putting ourselves out there. When we don't combat these destructive lies with truth, we end up believing them and creating false versions of ourselves—curated, filtered versions, the best versions, the versions that we think people must want. In the process, we end up lopping off all our undesirable parts, boxing them up, and hiding them away. We fear that if anyone knew us truly and fully, they wouldn't want us. So we give them the version of ourselves we think they want instead of who we really are. We try so hard to be someone who's lovable, someone else, someone not us, only to discover that no matter how hard we try, we're still lonely, feeling unknown and unloved. This is where those looping lies take us. They may seem like inconsequential things, even helpful things at times, but their result is our own disappointment. Even if we figure out how to spot them, how do we ever get off the merry-go-round?

We fear that if anyone knew us truly and fully, they wouldn't want us. So we give them the version of ourselves we think they want instead of who we really are.

You Can Take the Truth Off-Ramp

What if instead of a negative repetitive loop, you were on a positive repetitive loop? I mean, think about how different your life would look (or just your day) if you walked around believing you are known and wanted and loved? What if you really *believed* it deep down in your bones and lived like it was true? This is the goal of this chapter: to get you to a place where you walk confidently in the love and affirmation of God. And we are going to get there by learning and meditating on just one verse together. I included it at the very beginning of this chapter. Let's read it again: "See what great love the Father has lavished on us, that we should be called children of God! And that is what we are!" (1 John 3:1a).

This is it! This—God loves you with an extravagant, wondrous love, and he calls you his own. *This*—we're going to unpack this

47

truth and just sit in it for the rest of this chapter (and I hope for the rest of our lives). *This*—if we just get this one thing, if we really believe it and live in it, then we have a firm foundation for our lives. So let's go after it like our lives depend on it.

This Is Your Identity: Loved by God

Our verse tells us to "*see* what great love the Father has lavished on us" (1 John 3:1a, emphasis added). And this is precisely what we're going to do: see and understand that great love by diving into the context of our verse. We find our verse in a letter written by John to some of his church friends. And I can honestly think of no better person in the Bible to share about God's love for us than John. John knew firsthand about the love of God. He spent three years living with Jesus—working shoulder to shoulder with him, laughing with him, eating meals with him, learning from him, and just being with Jesus. By the time he wrote his gospel account, he called himself "the disciple whom Jesus loved" (John 21:7). Do you hear that?! This was how John identified himself—as *loved* by Jesus! Can you imagine if this was how you most deeply saw and identified yourself?

John wants us to know we are *loved.* He goes to great lengths to help his friends and us, his readers, understand God's extravagant love for us. And let me tell you one thing that should give you great hope—John isn't speaking these truths to people who have it all together and are doing just fine. In fact, maybe he keeps bringing it up *because* they don't feel very loved or lovable. They've been really struggling—struggling with real hardships and against lies that people have been spreading about their core beliefs and the  truth of Jesus. Sound familiar? John is modeling for us just exactly what we need to do when we come up against lies: fight them with the truth! So, let's keep on discovering more of this love that John so urgently wants his friends to believe in.

One thing you could do right now is read all of 1 John with an eye on his repetition of love and care. It's five short chapters and should take you about fifteen minutes. If you don't have time for that, just read chapter 3. If you don't have a Bible, just Google it. We're using the NIV translation if you want to read the version we're working from.

This Is the Truth John Shares about God's Love

God's Love Is Truly Great

As you read 1 John, did you see the prominence of God's love throughout John's letter? It's hard *not* to catch John's enthusiasm, isn't it? Even in our verse, notice we have two exclamation points. John is exclaiming his wonder at the greatness of God's lavish love for us! In the original language (Greek), his excitement is even more evident. Expert theologian Dr. Robert Yarbrough says there's one word translators haven't fully captured and we "domesticate it down" and don't express the fullness of John's exhilaration. He says the first word in our verse, *see*, should be a *whoa!* with another exclamation point (that'd make three). His translation would read: "Whoa! What kind of love has the Father given to us that we're called children of God!" Dr. Yarbrough says that John is "grabbing you by the lapel, getting in your face" in order to communicate his passion and enthusiasm that the God of the universe has made us his own children![1] This is what I want you to catch from John: a fanatical exuberance about God's love—a love that's so astounding you can hardly contain yourself, a love so earth-shattering that it changes you to the core. This is the love John is talking about, a love we simply must find out more about!

God's Love Is Shown Fully in Jesus

God expresses his love to us in so many ways: in the beauty of nature, in providing us with everything we need, in answering our prayers. But his love is most fully, extravagantly, and beautifully expressed in Jesus. In his letter, John tells his friends this on repeat, saying:

- *"This is how we know what love is*: Jesus Christ laid down his life for us" (1 John 3:16a, emphasis added).
- *"This is how God showed his love among us*: He sent his one and only Son into the world that we might live through him" (1 John 4:9, emphasis added).
- *"This is love*: not that we loved God, but that he loved us and sent his Son as an atoning sacrifice for our sins" (1 John 4:10, emphasis added).

Do you hear that repetition? This is love, this is love, this is love. And who is this love? *Jesus.* This is love: *Jesus*—God's perfect Son, who gave his own life to save ours. This is love: *Jesus*—who deserved only worship and reverence, but instead endured every shame, every humiliation, every violence in our place. This is love: *Jesus*—God in the flesh, of infinite worth, who paid a measureless price to make us daughters and sons of God. This is love: not that we loved God but that he loved us and sent his Son to take our place. This is love: *Jesus.* Do you hear it? Do you maybe want to read all that again? Go ahead. Let it really sink in. God loves you. Period. He gave his most valuable gift, Jesus, so that you might know and experience the full extravagance of his boundless love. This is how we know love: we know Jesus.

God's Love Is Not Dependent on Us

Here's the most amazing part of all this: God's love doesn't depend on you or me. Like John says, "This is love: not that we loved God, but that he loved us and sent his Son as an atoning sacrifice for our sins" (1 John 4:10). God doesn't love us because we loved him first. No, he is the one who initiated this love. He doesn't love us because we are good or right or perfect. Jesus didn't die for the godly, but the *un*godly (Romans 5:6). *Whew!* I don't know about you, but this is

Do You Know God's Love?

Have you experienced the radical, sacrificial love of God in Jesus? Maybe you have and you're all in, longing to keep diving deeper. Maybe you've felt this love in the past, but right now you're feeling all dried up. Or possibly you're just dipping your toe in the water. Wherever you're coming from, let me just be clear on this one point:

There is nothing for you to do but to receive it.

Jesus has already done all the work. Like John says, it's not about you loving God but God loving you and making a way for you to experience his love through Jesus. All you have to do is embrace Jesus. John says elsewhere, "To all who did receive [Jesus], to those who believed in his name, he gave the right to become children of God" (John 1:12).

- *If you've never taken this step*, it's as simple as telling Jesus, "I receive your love. I believe you laid down your life for me. Forgive my sins. Make me yours and I will be yours."
- *If you believe this*, if you've made Jesus yours, but right now you find yourself far off, there is no shame or judgment here. Jesus's arms are open wide, waiting for you. Just tell him, "Jesus, bring me near again. Forgive my wandering. Help me feel and experience your love for me."
- *If you're at a good place*, here are words for you: "O Lord, store up in me a vast depth of your love that I might draw upon the next time I feel far away from you."

This is my hope—that you would know God's extravagant affection, not just in your head but deep in your heart, so that you would say with honest joy and wonder, *Whoa!* "What great love the Father has lavished on us, that we should be called children of God! And that is what we are!" (1 John 3:1a).

seriously good news for a mess maker like me. Not that I go around *trying* to sin! I am always trying to do just the opposite! *And* so often failing. Thankfully, God's love doesn't depend on my trying, earning, or succeeding! In fact, he is all grace every time I mess up and ask his forgiveness. His patience never wears thin, his mercies never run out. His love isn't dependent on us but on his own desire for us, a desire so strong that he would sacrifice his Son to make us his own.

God's Love Is As Safe As He Is

John tells us that God's love is a love that we can "know and rely on" (1 John 4:16). His love is as safe and reliable as he is. You see, God isn't just loving as a part of his moral character, rather it is intrinsic to who he is, inextricably tied up with his very person. John says, "God *is* love" (1 John 4:8, emphasis added). In other words, love is the very essence of who he is. He is the standard of love, the very definition of love. When we want to know what love is like, we must look at God. And his love is a love like him—boundless, constant, eternal, free, complete. This is the love we need, isn't it? A good and safe love, a dependable love that doesn't depend on us, a love that doesn't wax or wane, a love that we could never lose. This is the love of God for all who believe in him. This is his love for you and me.

God's Love Is Lavish!

That's what our memory verse tells us! Isn't it the most amazing thought that someone loves you *lavishly*, not because of anything you've done or not done? Someone who knows you intimately—all the good, all the bad, all those "unlovable" parts you boxed up and hid away—and yet he loves you just the same? You are never unloved or unlovable to God. He wants the as is, unfiltered version of you. His love doesn't waver when you fail. His love doesn't increase when you perform. Do you hear that? You need to hear that! God doesn't love you more when you go to church or help people or do good stuff. God doesn't ditch you when you ditch him. Even when we are faithless, he is faithful. Always. His love is faithful because God can't be anything but himself (2 Timothy 2:13). You need a love like that—a love that is too radical, too wonderful, too good—the *lavish* love of God. It's a love that draws you back when you wander because you long for it while you're away, knowing it will always be there. It's a love that only increases your love for him and your desire to follow him and become more like him. This is the love of God. *Whoa!* "What great love the Father has *lavished* on us, that we should be called children of God! And that is what we are!" (1 John 3:1a, emphasis added).

Someone Loves the Uncut, Unfiltered, Uncurated Version of You

An Open Letter to Anyone Who Feels Unlovable

Oh friend,

I see you. Struggling, with your mask firmly in place, smile drawn on. You make light, though you're heavy—weighed down with the weariness of trying, trying, trying. Trying to be someone—someone interesting, someone cool, someone smart, someone not you. Will anyone ever know you? The uncut, unfiltered, uncurated version? The true you?

Do you still remember *that* you? Smudged cheeks, a song in your heart, mismatched, wild, uncaring, and unaware? Before the world checked you. Before you saw others as things to become. Before insecurity settled in and made you doubt. Before anxiety told you to worry. Before you hated your skin, your tummy, your laugh, the sound of your own voice. Where did it go? Where is your song? Where are you?

You're in there still—waiting, waiting, waiting. Waiting for the safe person, the safe place, a home where you can unpack all those parts of yourself you boxed up. Sometimes I see a glimpse—the honest you. You're in there. Just holding your breath.

But this world isn't safe. It never will be. You learned it young and learned it well. It says be yourself, but be the you who is a little more like this or that, a little prettier, a little bolder, a little more successful, the "best version" of you. You've learned that people love you because and people love you when. So you contorted yourself into the world's mold, lopping off the undesirable pieces of yourself so you could fit in. Where you were too much, you became less. And where you were not enough, you strived to become. But still you found yourself imperfect and unlovable.

If only there were a person who loved you as is—a home where you were always welcome, always loved. Not loved *because* or loved *when*, just *loved*. A home where you can hang your mask and leave it off. A place where you can be accepted, fully known, with all your flaws and failings, and yet fully loved. Could such a place exist? Is it possible you were made for it, and that is why you long for it so desperately?

Yes. There is.

There's a home for you. I know because I've been there. And that home is a person: Jesus. He doesn't love you because you're lovable, but even when you aren't. He doesn't love you when you perform, but even when you fail. His love is unwavering, because he is unwavering—a firm foundation for the true you. You see, he loves all the things you've learned to hate—your skin, your laugh, your tummy, the sound of your voice. He loves your song and wants to hear you sing it. He loves all those parts you boxed up. He wants them all. He wants the uncut, unfiltered, uncurated version of you. The true you. Because he made you, every single bit. And he loves you radically, completely, without end. And when you come to him confessing your falseness and failings, he exchanges them for mercy and love, kindness and compassion. He bore your imperfections to give you his perfections. Where you were too much or not enough, he was always just right. You don't have to strive anymore or wear that mask. You don't have to wait anymore. Your home is here, and he's welcoming you in. Always. If you've never been, or if you've been wandering a while, the door is open. The door is always open. His arms are always open. Always.

Won't you go in?

*This was originally written on the *Dwell Differently* blog. We received such an overwhelming response, we wanted to share it with you. DwellDifferently.com/blogs /bible-memory/someone-loves-the-uncut-unfiltered-un-curated-version-of-you

God's Love Is Not Only Infinite, It's Intimate

Like we've already begun to discover, God's love is a whole new category of love. God's love isn't just great in the sense that it's infinite but also because it's intimate—so intimate, in fact, that it's difficult to wrap our minds around. God loves us with the devoted love of a father. Our verse tells us it was his love that compelled him to adopt us as his own children. John is so excited about it that he repeats it, saying, "That is what we are!" (1 John 3:1a). As a parent myself,

I understand something of this love. I truly love my kids; I'm constantly thinking about them, helping them, caring for them, serving them, hoping and planning good things for them. Yet, my greatest expressions of love fall desperately short of God's parental love for us. His perfect parental love never loses patience or falsely accuses or gets totally worn-out. In this, I am amazed. *Whoa!* What great love!

But wait, there's more! There's a whole other level to God's intimacy, where we have no human equivalent. God is so intimate with us that he actually lives in us. John says, "If anyone acknowledges that Jesus is the Son of God, God lives in them and they in God" (1 John 4:15). Even if we've heard this before, is it not just too much to wrap our minds around? God himself lives in us, guiding us, convicting us, helping us say *no* to selfishness and sin and *yes* to him and his good ways. God loves us so intimately that he is ever present with us, giving us everything we need for life and godliness (2 Peter 1:3).

This is just some of what John says about God's love. It's why John uses all the exclamation points he can find to say, *Whoa!* "What great love the Father has lavished on us, that we should be called children of God! And that is what we are!" (1 John 3:1a).

I don't know if I'll ever say *see* instead of *whoa!* again. Whoa! What a truly great love God has given us! He is too good, too wonderful, too gracious to love us like he does. I hope studying this verse has been a new and deeper revelation of that love. It has been for me. And if you follow Jesus, you can recite this truth over yourself in bold assurance that God loves you with an unchanging, extravagant, intimate love. It's a love you cannot earn or deserve yet were given all the same. It's a love that finds its foundation in the person and work of Jesus. It's the love you long for and the only love you'll ever need. Indeed, you are loved. My prayer is that you would experience this love more and more as you memorize and meditate on our memory verse.

Apply the TRUTH

Now it's your turn to do the work! I've listed some prompts to help you identify where you're at and where you might need growth.

- What do you most need to hear and believe about God's love for you? Dependability, extravagance, acceptance, intimacy?
- What are some of *your* negative loops—the reasons you feel unlovable, unworthy, unwanted?
- How are you protecting yourself by presenting a curated version of yourself?
- What is one way this verse specifically combats one of the lies you believe about being unlovable?
- Try catching yourself in a negative loop today, and tell yourself this verse instead. Try to make a habit of reciting this verse to yourself anytime you feel unlovable or unwanted.
- How are you trying to earn God's love?
- Is there something that you feel so much shame about that you doubt God's love for you? Confess it to him. In Christ, all your sins are forgiven. You can walk in the full freedom of his love.
- Read 1 John 4:7–21 and spend some time just meditating on God's love.
- Listen to the podcast episode for this chapter, where Vera and I talk about how this verse has impacted our lives.

Go to the podcast here!

S
WG
LTFH
LOUTW
SBCCOG
ATIWWA♛

1J3.1A

SEE WHAT GREAT LOVE THE FATHER HAS LAVISHED ON US,
THAT WE SHOULD BE CALLED CHILDREN OF GOD!
AND THAT IS WHAT WE ARE!
I JOHN 3:1A

BUT BLESSED IS THE ONE WHO TRUSTS IN THE LORD, WHOSE CONFIDENCE IS IN HIM.
JEREMIAH 17:7

BBITOWTITL
WCIIH J17.7

4

TRUTH When You Feel INSECURE

NATALIE

But blessed is the one who trusts in the LORD, whose confidence is in him.

—Jeremiah 17:7

Instagram Knows I'm Getting Older

When I scroll my feed, all my ads are "hacks to stop aging" and tricks to help me "look super snatched." They promise me "the face and body of a twenty-year-old" if I'd just try this cream or download that app. And I find myself wondering where all the cute sweatshirts and jewelry went. But deep down, I already know the answer: Instagram ads are a window into my true self. They target me with these ads because I *am* aging, and they know it. Instagram *always* knows. But the deeper, harder truth is far more uncomfortable than the mere fact that I'm getting older: the algorithm was created to sell me more of what I want. It's designed to continually show me more and more of what I'm already looking at. The longer I pause, every time I swipe, whenever I click, Instagram knows it and shows me more of the same. So, what am I seeing? A mirror into myself and my desires. And it forces me to ask these

questions: Why am I pausing, swiping, and clicking on these promises to keep me young? Why are these ads drawing me in? What are they telling me?

I'm insecure.

When I look in the "Instagram ad mirror," I see a woman who is aging and feeling pretty unsure about it. I see a woman who worries that her face looks somewhat like a pug—laughable when I say it here, but true. I see a woman wondering if those vitamins and supplements really do help reduce fine lines. *Can face yoga really make me look twenty?* You see, the truth is, when it comes to getting older, I feel about as secure as I did in middle school, which was the last time my body did a massive hormone shift. Eeeeesh! And I guess I could blame my insecurities on those unstable hormones—and certainly they don't help—but I think there's something more dubious going on here. The process of aging shouldn't leave me wondering *Who am I?* and *Where did my confidence go?* There's got to be something deeper.

A Foundational Problem

And so, as unsettling as it is, I'm thankful for the "Instagram mirror." It forces me to think about what's really going on in me. And when I look beneath the surface, I find a shaky foundation, one I didn't realize I was even building on: my looks. I feel ridiculous confessing this as a forty-something lady. I mean, I have no delusions that I'm some sort of supermodel over here! What I'm talking about is this: I'm used to my face being *my* face, the same one I've had for decades now without much real change.

Recently though, every morning when I look in the mirror, it's a *Freaky Friday* experience, because I see *my mom* staring back at me! It's seriously startling. Now, don't get me wrong, I *love* my mom! She's a wonderful, beautiful woman, one who has aged *gracefully*, but she's a good twenty years older than me. And I can't help but wonder how I aged twenty years overnight every time I see my new "old" self in the mirror.

Sadly, every time I see that person in the mirror, I mostly just want to fix her, change her, or at least hide her flaws. Not good. Not right. And I know it. It's a problem. You see, I've put at least some degree of my confidence and identity in my looks, and they simply aren't a safe place or a firm foundation. I'm insecure about this new aging person, but at least now I know it and can address it. Now that I've bared my own fragile ego, I have to ask you something.

> Sadly, every time I see that person in the mirror, I mostly just want to fix her, change her, or at least hide her flaws. Not good. Not right. And I know it. It's a problem.

What about You?

You're going to need to take an honest inventory of your own foundation if this chapter is going to be of any value to you at all. Now, at first glance, you may say that you're building your confidence on the foundation of Jesus. And I sincerely hope so! That'd be my knee-jerk response too. But sometimes we find we don't have both feet as firmly planted on the foundation of Jesus as we first thought. Maybe we have one foot on something else, something that feels shaky and unsettling to us. So, forgive me if I force you to poke around a bit to see just how secure your footing really is. Consider these questions, and really let them sink in.

What are the ads on *your* socials telling you?

What makes you feel confident? A relationship? Your looks? Your bank account? Your smarts? Your success? Your status?

What makes you feel unsettled, shaky, precarious? Any of those same things?

What negative thoughts about your significance cycle through your mind late into the night?

What areas of your life make you feel like everything depends on you, like it would all fall apart without you?

Well. What did you find? Were there any foundation problems—things you didn't realize you were building on? Me too. What's totally ridiculous is how answering self-reflective questions always surprises me—like I somehow thought I had it all together until I answered a few simple questions. Maybe you're a little more self-aware than I am, maybe you already had a pretty good idea of what your insecurities and false foundations are, and maybe you weren't a bit caught off guard. But whether you were surprised or not, whether there was a lot there or only a little, we all have this one truth in common:

We all have ongoing foundation problems.

None of us have arrived. We're all constantly putting at least one toe on shaky ground. We're looking to a relationship, our looks, our current or future successes, our finances, our new sneakers or new house, our intellect, our charisma, you name it, we all have *something* that we're depending on to make us feel confident and secure.

Shaky Foundations

Whether our confidence is based in ourselves or it is placed in something outside ourselves, all of us rely at least to some degree on things we know aren't foolproof, things that aren't lasting or reliable or firm. And when we ignore or avoid this reality, insecurity lurks about the edges of our minds, whispering our deepest fear: at any moment, everything could all come tumbling down. These are the negative thoughts that plague us, making us feel insecure.

- If our confidence is based on our beauty, we will fight to keep it, protect it, and enhance it, and as it fades, we will wonder where our worth went.
- If our security is founded in our intellect, then we will always fear that someone will expose our ignorance.
- If our confidence is found in our finances, then every dip in the market is a dip in our sense of security.
- If our success is our foundation, then we will always strive to justify ourselves with ever-increasing performance.
- If our deepest foundation is in our relationships, then losing them is our deepest insecurity.

Do you see any of these tendencies in yourself? We know from experience that none of these things are dependable, lasting, or secure, don't we? And so our lives feel precarious, and we are insecure. "But blessed is the one who trusts in the LORD, whose confidence is in him" (Jeremiah 17:7).

Did you hear that? There is a right and good place for our confidence. There is a solid foundation, and that foundation is the Lord. Unlike ourselves, our relationships, or our circumstances, God is unchanging, safe, and dependable—the only stable and right foundation for our lives. And when we put our trust in the Lord, there is not only security but, like our verse tells us, there is true and lasting blessing. So let's dive into this verse and soak up every bit of it—the whole truth about the blessings available when we put our confidence in God.

Truth Triumphs over Insecurity

The Bad News First Though . . .

Our verse is a beautiful verse telling us about the blessings of trusting in God. But if we are going to be faithful to the truth of it, we must place it in its context, which is a sticky wicket. The people of God have abandoned him; they've planted their feet firmly on other foundations, which are not firm at all. Just prior to our verse, God reveals just exactly what they are trusting in, and it isn't him. They're trusting in themselves and other humans, trusting in what they can see and feel and touch, trusting that they can provide and achieve and win. And God tells them it is folly—there is no security or certainty in the plans and purposes of humans. There is no good thing for those whose hearts turn away from him, only a wasteland.

The Wasteland

God says that because they are trusting in other things, instead of experiencing joy and life and abundance in him, they are dried-up, withered versions of themselves. Hear what God says about those who turn away from him:

> This is what the LORD says:
> "Cursed is the one who trusts in man,
> who draws strength from mere flesh
> and whose heart turns away from the LORD.
> That person will be like a bush in the wastelands;
> they will not see prosperity when it comes.
> They will dwell in the parched places of the desert,
> in a salt land where no one lives."
>
> Jeremiah 17:5–6

That's a pretty bleak picture. God's people had turned their hearts away from him, and the results were disastrous. God tells his people, "When you try to find life in other things, there is no life at all. You are like a bush in the wasteland, dying from lack of water. There is no fruit, no growth. When you walk away from me, you are walking into the desert, a dried-up land where there is no good thing." God paints this stark picture as a warning of the reality of life without him. And that warning isn't just for God's people way back then. This is true for us still today. When we trust anything other than God, we find ourselves in a barren wasteland. There is nothing to satisfy our need, no prosperity, no good fruit, no place for us to grow and thrive. Instead, we're left wanting and weary. It is a pitiful picture, one I have experienced in my own life far too many times.

It Gets Worse before It Gets Better

Unfortunately, we aren't done with the bad news yet. You see, not only are the people of God wasting away in a desert place, but they've actually convinced themselves that everything is just fine. *What?!* How is that possible? God tells his people that all human hearts have this capacity to trick us into thinking everything is okay when everything is not okay. God says later in this same passage that our hearts are "deceitful above all things and beyond cure" (Jeremiah 17:9). So, not only are God's people shriveling up in a wasteland, but they're also believing that everything is perfectly fine. Can you relate? I can. I can't even count the times I've been in the desert, believing all the while that I'm in the mirage—convincing myself, "It's fine. I'm fine. Everything is fine," when everything is *not* fine!

> **I can't even count the times I've been in the desert, believing all the while that I'm in the mirage—convincing myself, "It's fine. I'm fine. Everything is fine," when everything is *not* fine!**

It's all too real.

My heart is no different from God's people in Jeremiah's time. And neither is yours. Our hearts truly are cunning and callous tricksters, convincing us we're gonna be okay. It's our hearts that justify us when we're clearly in the wrong. Our hearts defend our actions while blaming others, downplaying the damage or denying our part entirely. We want what we want, and we don't want anyone to tell us we're doing something wrong—not someone else, not our conscience, not even God. Like God's people of old, like all humans for all time, we often build our lives on shaky foundations, and our hearts convince us we're doing just fine.

God Will Not Stand By and Let His Children Waste Away

Like the good Father that he is, God refuses to let his children continue in their folly. We see this play out in the story we're following. God sends Jeremiah to wake his people up to their self-deception and lead them out of the desert of their waywardness. Jeremiah speaks the truth plainly to them, revealing the harsh reality of their situation. He warns them if they do not heed his words and turn their hearts back to God, God will take drastic measures to wake them up out of their delusion and save them out of their sin by means of his punishment.

For years and years God sends Jeremiah (and he isn't the only one) to hold out before them this warning of impending punishment for staying on their wrong course and the promise of blessing if they would turn and follow him. Despite all of this, God's people do not return to him with repentant hearts and reform their ways. Instead, they resolutely dive headlong into their choices to ignore and abandon God and his blessing. So finally, God gives them over to the things they've trusted in—their own selves and the military might of other nations—but their wisdom proves folly and their strength is exposed for weakness. A stronger, more powerful army comes and conquers them, taking them into captivity for seventy years.

The Promise Is Still Good

If you read Jeremiah, you'll find that these are some of the bleakest times in the history of God's people. Even still, God does not abandon them, and his promise of blessing still stands. The promise he held out from the very first is still good—if they will only return to him. Despite all their failings, despite their unswerving denials, God's promise never fails, because God never goes back on his word. Though God does punish his children, his punishment is not final judgment but punishment with a purpose: *restoration*. Even after all they've done, God longs for his children to return; he longs to bless them and be with them. He longs for their well-being and life. He longs for them to wake up to the truth of the wasteland and to come into the promises of life with him. Hear the promise of restoration in our verse and the ones following:

> But blessed is the one who trusts in the LORD,
> whose confidence is in him.
> They will be like a tree planted by the water
> that sends out its roots by the stream.
> It does not fear when heat comes;
> its leaves are always green.
> It has no worries in a year of drought
> and never fails to bear fruit.
>
> Jeremiah 17:7–8

God is calling them to *this*: to the security and confidence and abundance that comes from him. Remember the withered bush—fruitless, futile, parched, and planted in shifting sand? How different is the image here! When God's children trust him, they're like a deeply rooted tree planted by the water, drawing its life from the stream. They won't fear the blazing heat of trials that would otherwise shrivel them up. They have "no worries" in the drought, for they have a never-ending source of life-giving water. And this tree never "fails to bear fruit." This is a beautiful picture of the abundant blessing God offers his people.

This Blessing Is for Us!

This blessing isn't just for those rebels way back then, it's for us right now. God rescues sinners, even at our lowest possible

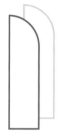

point—having run headlong into sin and sitting in the consequences of all our stupid choices. This is the message I need! Surely, I find myself sitting in the corner ashamed of myself far too often to admit! And I need to know that even God's discipline is for my ultimate redemption! I need to know that even in the midst of discipline, he's patiently holding out forgiveness, waiting for me to just turn and embrace him. This is the kind of God that reckless, headstrong sinners like me need. What about you? Do you ever find yourself far off, worn-out, and ashamed of the mess you've made? Unsure if God would want you back? I want you to hear this.

No matter how far you've wandered, it is never too far for God.
There's no sin you carry that Jesus hasn't already paid for.
There's no stain of shame that Jesus can't wash away.
There's no shaky foundation you've stood on (even for years) that disqualifies you.
There's no negative thought you've believed that can keep you from the truth of God's love for you.

Did you hear that?! God *loves* you! He still wants you, longs for you, calls you back to himself. He's gone to incredible lengths to make you his own.

You might just now be realizing that you've been self-deceived, wandering in a wasteland that is no oasis, trying to build your foundation on shifting sand. God is right there, waiting to forgive you and embrace you. His promise is for you. His goodness is for you. He wants you to live a fruitful, purposeful life, one full of blessing and joy, one that is secure, even in the midst of trial, want, or hardship. He is the firm foundation you can build your life on. So, dear one, root yourself in the truth of God. Put these words in your heart; keep them before you until you know them fully and can draw your confidence from the right source.

"But blessed is the one who trusts in the LORD, whose confidence is in him" (Jeremiah 17:7).

Apply the TRUTH

- What are your shaky foundations? Where are you out in the wasteland trying to pull life-giving water out of dry sand?
- Where might your heart be deceiving you? Where are you telling yourself everything is fine, when you know deep down it isn't?
- Where do you need to root your confidence in God?
- What specific blessings do you think would result from trusting God in those areas?
- When negative thoughts of insecurity crop up in your day (or night), say Jeremiah 17:7 over yourself.
- Listen to this chapter's podcast episode to hear us talk about the insecurities we struggle with.

Identity Activity

We are always tempted to base our identity and build our lives on things other than God. I want you to think about your life, all the things that make up who you are and what you do. I want you to envision them all piled up together in one big mass.

- Imagine all your responsibilities: your job, your schooling, and the pressures to succeed, to make money, and to live up to expectations.
- Imagine all your relationships: the people you know, the people you should call, the people who are hard, the people who are fun, the people you rely on, the people who rely on you.
- Imagine your status: what you have, what people think about you, the likes on your socials, what you wear, what you drive, what you do, what brings you pride, and what brings you shame.
- Imagine yourself: your hopes and dreams and successes, your fears and worries and failures, the life of your mind, you in the quiet spaces, you in the crowd, your personality, what makes you laugh, and what makes you weep.
- Imagine everything else: whatever isn't on this list, ask God to bring those things to mind.

Now look at your massive pile. Does it feel weighty, unstable, like it might just topple over? Just looking at my pile puts fear in my veins and pressure on my chest. Now imagine climbing up that pile and trying to build a home for yourself there. This is what we are doing—trying to find our security and safe home on top of things that will only tumble.

Now I want you to let all those things go for just a minute. Let go of all the expectations, all the shame, all the successes and failures, every burden to be and to do—let them go. Let go of all the things that you carry like they all depend on you. Let go of the worry and the fear that it all might come crashing down. Imagine yourself all by yourself, the essence of who you are. It's just you.

This is what God says to you: I love you.

I see you. I know you. All of you. I know your everything. All of it. And I love you. I see you trying to hold it all together, lying to yourself, saying everything is okay. And still, I love you. I see your poor choices, I see you wandering in the wasteland. And still, I love you. Would you come to me and give me your burdens? Would you let me make it right? Would you rest in my love? Would you put down roots in me? Would you take the life and blessing I offer? Would you let my love for you be your greatest joy and deepest foundation? When you find your identity in me, there is blessing. When you are confident in me, there is security. I love you. Would you come?

BUT BLESSED IS THE ONE WHO TRUSTS IN THE LORD, WHOSE CONFIDENCE IS IN HIM.
JEREMIAH 17:7

BBITOWTITL
WCIIH J17.7

FIIBGYHBSTF
ATINFYIITGOG
E2.8

FOR IT IS BY GRACE
YOU HAVE BEEN SAVED,
THROUGH FAITH—
AND THIS IS NOT
FROM YOURSELVES,
IT IS THE GIFT OF GOD.
EPHESIANS 2:8

5

TRUTH When You Feel UNACCEPTED

VERA

For it is by grace you have been saved, through faith—and this is not from yourselves, it is the gift of God.

—Ephesians 2:8

Accepted or Unaccepted?

When I hear the word *accepted*, the first thing that pops into my head is that little red icon on my Facebook notifications. Someone has requested to be your friend, and you can either confirm or delete their request. In the advent of Facebook, as an eighteen-year-old, I can remember how nerve-racking the *friending* game could feel. When I sent a friend request to someone I'd met in class or at practice, I was essentially betting on myself. I was betting that I'd been kind enough, that I was clever enough, that I'd made a good impression, and that my profile pic was on point.

Now, most friend requesting and accepting wasn't that big of a deal, because for the most part, people are quick to accept a friend request on social media from someone they've met. But say you had a crush on someone, say you thought they were cute and maybe just a bit out of your league, or maybe you hadn't gotten to know them that well yet, well then, yes, hitting that little request button was quite vulnerable. You were really putting yourself out there! I can remember scheming with my roommate about sending friend requests to boys we'd met in class. And then we'd sit around on our laptops (this was before smartphones) refreshing the page, waiting to see if we'd been accepted or not. It's a trivial example, but isn't this just the way the world operates? We put our best foot forward, and we wait to see if we are accepted or rejected.

What Happens When We Friend God?

I know this may sound like a funny question. But really. How do we see ourselves measuring up? Do we expect him to accept or reject us? If we were to make that bold move and send a request to God—who is all seeing, all knowing, and perfectly perfect—I think many of us believe we wouldn't be accepted. Because the truth is, we know us. We know all the ways we don't measure up, all the ways we aren't good enough for God. We are reminded of a thousand things keeping us from him:

Past sin
Current patterns of sin
An impatient and frustrated spirit
Negative thoughts
A selfish attitude

Things we should have done but didn't do

Laziness and apathy toward life and God himself

A lustful heart

Uncaring or deceitful words

A me-first lifestyle

Now, the world will tell you that you are a mostly good person and that you can accept yourself just the way you are—you don't need anyone else to accept you if you accept you. But you know you, just like I know me. And I know that I am not *mostly* good; in fact, I'm far from it. I know that I am mostly selfish, and I like things my own way. Yet even when it comes to my own way, I regularly come up short of my standard for how I should live my life (not even taking into consideration God's standard). I know all my failures as a mom and a wife and a friend and a coworker. I know the way I elevate my needs above those around me. I know that even in my service, I'm looking for recognition and applause. I know how my heart can be cold and my thoughts self-centered. So when I think of a holy, perfect God, if *I'm* not even good with me, how am I ever going to be good enough for God?

That Is Some Bad News Right There

You might be thinking, *Dang! I thought this chapter was going to give me truth to fight my negative thoughts of unacceptance, but all of this just confirms what I already thought: I really am unaccept-able.* And you wouldn't be totally wrong, *but* you also wouldn't be alone. This is the hard reality for all of us. "There is no one who does good, not even one" (Romans 3:12). None of us measures up. No one has arrived. No one is perfect. Every one of us has the same inherent problem: we are sinful people.

Since the beginning, since Adam and Eve ate the forbidden fruit, we have been coming up short. We prefer our own ideas, our own rights, our own desires over what God has laid out for us. And because God is holy and perfect, he cannot accept us. We have no way of friending God. We deserve his rejection—our friend request deleted. Just before the verse we are memorizing in this chapter, in Ephesians 2, Paul lays out our sin problem pretty succinctly:

We are "dead in [our] transgressions and sins" (v. 1).
We have "followed the ways of this world" (v. 2).
We gratify "the cravings of our flesh" (v. 3).
We follow our own "desires and thoughts" (v. 3).
We are "by nature deserving of wrath" and are sinful (v. 3).

Man. That's pretty hard. No wonder we are on the outs with God. But as bleak as our problem is, it's only when we correctly diagnose an illness that we can find the remedy.

Accepted

We Need a Remedy—We Want to Be Accepted

Now, if you know Jesus or if you've heard about him in the last few chapters, you already know the solution to our sin problem, and it's the gospel (which is shorthand for the good news about Jesus). With all this bad news, aren't you ready for some good news?! I want to show you how the gospel specifically addresses our "unaccepted" status. If the bad news is that we are unaccepted, the good news is this: God still wants us! He loves us and longs to be in relationship with us.

He wants to say *yes* to our friend request!

So, God did everything we could not do to make that possible. He sent his Son, Jesus, to be acceptable in our place. Jesus lived up to God's perfect standard—he lived a sin-free life, never failing, always serving, always humble, always kind, always speaking truth, full of perfect peace and justice, always lifting up the marginalized, always keeping God on his rightful throne. Jesus did what we could never do. And then he did the most incredible thing for anyone who would believe in him: he took our penalty, dying in our place and putting all our sins to death on the cross. And in exchange for our sins, he gave us his righteous and accepted standing with God. And this was all God's plan from the beginning. The Bible says it this way: "God made him who had no sin to be sin for us, so that in him we might become the righteousness of God" (2 Corinthians 5:21). What does this tell us? God wants us. As unacceptable as our behavior may be, God still wants us. He went to radical lengths to prove it.

The ball is in your court.

And if you are listening right now to what I'm saying, then there is something sitting in your notifications: a little red icon, a friend request *from Jesus*. It isn't that you've sent him a friend request. No, it is quite the opposite. Jesus has sent you a request and is asking you to accept him—to accept that he has done all of this on your behalf. You don't have to make excuses for your faults or try to be good enough. He's already taken care of your sin problem. You don't have to prove yourself to him; he already knows all of it, and wants you just the same. The question is, do you want him? If you do, if you accept Jesus, something amazing happens: God becomes your friend too because you have a mutual friend, Jesus. Anyone who is a friend of Jesus is a friend of his Father, automatically (John 13:20). If you accept Jesus, then you are accepted by God. This is the gospel—not that we can do anything to friend God and be accepted by him, but that he friends us and accepts us because of Jesus. "This is love: not that we loved God, but that he loved us and sent his Son as an atoning sacrifice [acceptable payment] for our sins" (1 John 4:10). God is the one who initiated the relationship and made it possible by taking care of our unacceptable status and making us acceptable in Christ.

> **This is the gospel—not that we can do anything to friend God and be accepted by him, but that he friends us and accepts us because of Jesus.**

I know this is a long metaphor. I also know that it's somewhat cheesy. But I don't really care. You can't tell me you wouldn't lose your mind if you woke up one morning and Denzel Washington or Taylor Swift or the president or (fill in your biggest hero here) had requested to be friends with you. Could you imagine?! "Why in the world would Denzel friend *me*?" Your mind would rightfully be blown. Now imagine, then, an open friend request from King Jesus. This religion, Christianity, is the only religion where God stoops from his throne as Creator, King, gloriously high above the heavens, way down here to our lowly place and seeks to friend and accept otherwise unacceptable humans. This is completely upside-down! Why would any God do that?! Every other religion requires the human to do all the right things and be all the right things in order to maybe, just maybe, be accepted by God or reach some state of perfection. But by his great, deep, rich, overflowing, wild love, our God recognizes our complete inability to be perfect and instead makes us perfect in his Son. Our God loves us and seeks us and makes a way for us! And what can we do to earn that? Nothing. Not one single thing. God has done everything for us. To be friends with him, all we need to do is merely accept his request.

As all-out mind-blowing as it sounds, it's true!

Man, as I sit in this Starbucks, I'm thinking about how *maybe* even one person reading this just had it hit for the first time. *Maybe* one person just realized what God is actually offering you. He is reaching for you, wherever you are, no matter how far off. He wants a relationship with you—one that isn't based on your striving or performing or perfection, one that isn't hindered by your failings or your past or your problems. His love and acceptance are rooted in his unchanging goodness, mercy, and love. And he is offering all of that to you. You just have to accept it. And if you're feeling like that's you right now, at this moment, hi, hi, hi! Can I just pray for you?

God, this is my friend. Would you be near them in this moment? Help them to sit in this clear state of mind, seeing for the first time what you offer them: acceptance. I pray you'd give them the courage to accept Jesus right now. Give them strength of heart and confidence that you are good, you are love, and you want them. Thank you for reaching for us, God. Thank you for Jesus.

Accepted through Faith

All of this is on offer for us. The love and grace and acceptance of God . . . all of it. And all we must do is turn from our wayward ways and believe that Jesus is who God says he is—the Savior King who will forgive us and bring us into forever relationship with him.

"For it is by grace you have been saved, through faith" (Ephesians 2:8a). Easy peasy, right? But what if that faith part *is* the hard part? What if you struggle to believe? What if having faith feels like another thing that you have to do in order to get to God? Oh, hello. I've been there too.

Can I tell you a quick story about how I came to follow Jesus?

When I was eight, my sister Natalie became a Christian. She was in college, and she came home one weekend and told me all about Jesus. I'd heard of him, I had a Bible, and as a worrisome little kid, I actually read the thing. Well, Natalie told me all about Jesus and asked me if I wanted to follow him. It was an easy yes! I wanted so badly to be right with God. Mature beyond my years, I had actually thought about these things plenty of times. So when Natalie told me all I needed to do was accept Jesus, I was in. I felt that immediate

79

relief and joy that come with accepting Jesus. What a beautiful thing! When I think back to my younger kid-self, I'm hopeful for the children in my life, that they might be set free at a young age! The only problem was that for the next several weeks, I wondered . . . *Did I really do it? Did I say the right thing? Did I pray right? Did I have enough faith?* You see, I'd put all of it back on me. And then one night, I stumbled across this verse: "Truly I tell you, if you have faith as small as a mustard seed, you can say to this mountain, 'Move from here to there,' and it will move. Nothing will be impossible for you" (Matthew 17:20).

This passage comes after the disciples had been trying to heal a man but couldn't. Even the disciples didn't always have enormous faith. But Jesus tells them in the midst of their own faith crisis that they don't need monumental faith, just teeny-tiny faith. I remember reading it and thinking to myself, *I have that tiny mustard seed! I don't have a big faith, but I do have that mustard seed! And if I have faith so small, but can move a mountain, then it is a good enough faith!* Why? As Tim Keller puts it, "It is not the strength of your faith but the object of your faith that actually saves you."[1]

Let me just give you one more encouragement in this. Whenever my faith feels weak, I always remind myself of this story in the Bible. A father brings his son who's been tormented by an evil spirit to the disciples, who again are unable to help. When Jesus arrives on the scene, the father asks Jesus to heal his boy, *if he can.* Jesus says, "'If you can'? . . . Everything is possible for one who believes" (Mark 9:23). Immediately the boy's father responds, "I do believe; help me overcome my unbelief!" (Mark 9:24). *Yes! This is me too. I do believe! O Jesus, help me overcome my unbelief!* God doesn't expect perfect faith from us. We can come honest and weak. Faith itself is a gift from God, just like his grace. So if faith is hard for you, like this father in the story, ask God to help you overcome your unbelief.

FIIBGYHBSTF
ATINFYIITGOG
E2.8

God, my faith is weak. It is small, like a tiny seed. But what faith I do have, I will put in you. And God, even while I have this faith, this tiny, almost immeasurable faith, I have loads and loads of unbelief right there next to it, threatening to overtake it. Will you help me with my unbelief? Help me, God. Give me faith to believe in Jesus, to accept him, and to live in the blessings of a life with you. I will keep messing up. And my faith won't be perfect. Will you forgive me? And will you strengthen my faith day by day? And in times of unbelief, will you help me believe more?

Accepted and Forgetful

I hesitated writing the first part of this chapter, because if you already follow Jesus, I thought that this might bore you. But what a lie! What a trick for me or you to believe that we are somehow past the gospel. Tim Keller says it this way:

> In our Christian life we never "get beyond the gospel" to something more advanced. The gospel is not the first step in a stairway of truths; rather, it is more like the hub in a wheel of truth. The gospel is not just the ABCs but the A to Z of Christianity. The gospel is not the minimum required doctrine necessary to enter the kingdom but the way we make all progress in the kingdom.[2]

Even though I follow Jesus and have walked with him for over two decades, I often forget the gospel. I might know and believe that I'm ultimately accepted before God, but I sometimes live an unaccepted reality. I'm spinning my wheels, making no progress at all. I try to work and earn and check off boxes and do good things for God—somehow trying to earn all over again what is already mine. I think this might be why Paul reminds the folks in Ephesus of who they were before Jesus and then points them to their moment of rescue and acceptance by Jesus. Why? Because they need the truth of Jesus's rescue just as much in their day-to-day lives as they did when they were first rescued. And so do we. Let me repeat here the beautiful and truthful words of our verse: "For it is by grace you have been saved, through faith—and this is not from yourselves, it is the gift of God" (Ephesians 2:8).

> I might know and believe that I'm ultimately accepted before God, but I sometimes live an unaccepted reality. I'm spinning my wheels, making no progress at all. I try to work and earn and check off boxes and do good things for God—somehow trying to earn all over again what is already mine.

So whoever you are—whether your eyes are only starting to open to your acceptance in Christ for the first time, or you've walked with Jesus for a lifetime, or you're still just working to figure it all out—God's grace, the free gift of salvation, and all it brings with it is for you. Free. Unearned. Unmerited. Available now, and every single day.

But you'll have to keep on remembering.

Can I say right here that it will need to be a regular practice for you to remember your acceptance. Why? Because it is so human to go back to putting ourselves in the middle of the story. For some of you, the burden of your past sin and current failure might threaten to keep you living like you are unaccepted. For others, like me, your perfectionist tendencies and need to achieve might keep you on a hamster wheel of performing as if you aren't accepted. It's so human to find ourselves in that negative loop we keep talking about. But know this: you can (and should!) always keep coming back to the gospel. You can refocus, remember, and put Jesus back at the center of the story. It is what he has done that has saved us. We can memorize this chapter's focus verse, dwell on it, believe it in our core, and speak it to ourselves daily—this truth is the starting point for living accepted every day.

Accepted and Blessed

When we accept Jesus, and therefore are accepted by God, we have a whole host of blessings available to us that go *way* beyond our immediate rescue and status as people who are reconciled to God. Yes, we have been saved from our sin, which is the ultimate gift of God, but he doesn't stop there. Let's look at the verses immediately surrounding our verse in Ephesians 2 to find out what else God gives us in Christ:

We are made alive in Christ (v. 5).
We are seated with Christ in the heavenly realms (v. 6).
We are brought near to God (v. 13).
We are granted peace (v. 17).
We are given access to the Father (v. 18).
We become members of God's household (v. 19).
We are citizens of heaven (v. 19).
We are standing on the shoulders of past believers (v. 20).
Christ is our cornerstone (v. 20).
We are a holy temple (v. 21).
God lives in us (v. 22).

That's a lot! How do I even begin? I could write a whole book just on these things God gives us when we're accepted by him, but two of them truly make my mind explode.

First, when we are accepted, we are raised up with Jesus and seated in the heavenly realms with him. Can we just imagine for one second the true, miraculous, mysterious reality that we are seated with Christ in the heavenly realms *like right now*?!

I want you to just take a minute and close your eyes and visualize this: You. Seated with Jesus. In heaven. When I stop and consider myself seated with Christ in the heavenly realms, it's a total perspective shift. I'm able to zoom way, way, way out from my everyday life and all the details of my circumstances and all my negative thoughts and feelings. I'm able instead to remember the greater spiritual reality that is happening all around me. If Christ is seated in the heavenly realms above all rule and authority and power and dominion and every title that can be given (Ephesians 1:21), and I am seated there with him (Ephesians 2:6), and I am blessed with *every* spiritual blessing in the heavenly realms (Ephesians 1:3), then I can also be victorious alongside Jesus because I have all I need in him. Again, he is the center of the story, carrying it all, and I am not. My tiny, zoomed-in world seems a whole lot different when I'm living in light of the zoomed-out spiritual reality. When I am accepted, I am also victorious with Christ, because of Christ. And this is true for everyone who believes in Jesus.

Second, not only is there this supernatural, outside-of-us, above-us, otherworldly thing going on because we are seated with Christ in the heavenly realms, but when we are accepted by God, we become a place where God lives, a holy temple, a home for God himself, right here in our very physical, right-now bodies. I wish I could put a mind-blown emoji right here . . . *Did you hear that?!* God, the same God who created everything out of nothing, the one who is all knowing, all powerful, and all loving, *lives in you* when you are accepted by him. This is no small thing to pass over. Those spiritual blessings in the heavenly realms? They are  unreal! And God in us? What a holy privilege, what a fall on your face, weep, and tremble kind of moment. God has made *us* a home for himself. Who or what could ever be against us (Romans 8:31)?

When we're accepted, we are victorious, and God lives in us, giving us everything we could ever need.

Accepted and Blessed to Be a Blessing

Let's keep reading the verses following our memory verse to discover another blessing that comes from being accepted by God through faith.

> For it is by grace you have been saved, through faith—and this is not from yourselves, it is the gift of God—not by works, so that no one can boast. For we are God's handiwork, created in Christ Jesus to do good works, which God prepared in advance for us to do.
>
> Ephesians 2:8–10

■ We Get to Do Good Works

Paul is telling us here that when we're saved by the work of God, we get to participate in his work in the world. This is where things get real good for me. Like I said previously, I love to do the thing, to work hard, to make plans, and to succeed. The problem isn't doing the good thing itself. Rather, my problem is doing those good things in an attempt to earn what I've already been given—God's grace. But when I have my mind lined up right, when Jesus is at the center of my story, when I remember the freeing truth that God's grace is not earned, then watch out world! I can do good work from the overflow of God's grace and in gratitude to him—not out of my own strength or for my glory or to win God's favor.

■ We Were Made for a Purpose

Did you see what else the text says? We are called God's *handiwork*. The original word used here can also be translated "work of art." I love thinking about God planning, dreaming, designing, and making me—his work of art—just the way he did, on purpose and *for a purpose*. God, in his sovereign, thoughtful, eternal ways, prepared and planned for me to work. I am meant to do worthy, right, and beautiful things in my time here on earth. I am called to create and put effort into the things God has specifically planned for me to do. Why?

■ We Get to Display God's Grace

When we accept Jesus, we display his grace in our lives. In Ephesians 2:7, Paul says that in us, God displays "the incomparable riches of his grace, expressed in his kindness to us in Christ Jesus." Every bit of goodness given to us displays his own glorious goodness. Every merciful act, every kindness, every ounce of love tells of this glorious God, who alone deserves worship and praise forever and ever. This God loves the unlovable, sees the overlooked, and stoops down to the lowly—it is a glorious mystery! This God rescues not because of what we do or have done but because of who he is, and who he is is glorious. And on that future day, when all is made right, when everything culminates in the eternal reign of God, we will all (and I mean people from every tribe and tongue and all of creation!) give glory to God for his great kindness expressed in his free gift of acceptance. The immeasurable riches of God's grace in his acceptance of us will be on display for all eternity (Ephesians 2:7). And even now, in your life, in your small sphere of influence, his grace is on display so that he might get the glory. And so we say, "To him be the glory! Amen!"

■ So, Let's Point Others to Jesus

When we do good things for others, we are testifying to the goodness of our God. Our good works shine his light in our dark world so that others might see Jesus in us and give glory to God (Matthew 5:16). Do you remember what was once true of you? Paul says in this same passage that you were without hope and without God in the world (Ephesians 2:12). This is the stark reality of so many of our friends, neighbors, strangers at the grocery store, and even our enemies who don't yet know Jesus—they are without hope and without God in the world, just like we once were. But our good works—our love and kindness, our words of truth, our very lives—sing out the beautiful news that God wants them too! We do good works not to earn God's favor, but to woo others to this God who has done everything to be in relationship with his people.

If God Accepts Me, Then I Am Acceptable—Period

When God accepts us, we are accepted once and for all, forever. I don't have to bet on myself ever again. I don't need to worry about being smart enough, or good enough, or kind enough, or charitable enough to make God like me or to get him to accept me. He just accepts me because of Jesus. Done. And what is more, when I am in Jesus, accepted as a friend of God, I can never, ever mess it up. Forever, I am accepted.

This means when I struggle with those negative thoughts that tell me I'm unaccepted or left out, I can get off that loop by reminding myself of this truth: if God accepts me, then I am acceptable. Period. It doesn't matter what other people think about me if the God of all things says I'm all good. I can let any judgment roll off. I don't have to stress about whether I measure up or if I'm cool enough or smart enough or successful enough. No worries here. My deepest reality is that I belong to God; I am his friend. And that is more than enough.

Final Thoughts

I could write some final thoughts here. I could summarize all I've said. But Paul says it better. I've mashed two of his prayers from his letter to the Ephesians into one, and it is my prayer for you. Hear these ancient words and let them wash over you with hope and love.

> I keep asking that the God of our Lord Jesus Christ, the glorious Father, may give you the Spirit of wisdom and revelation, so that

you may know him better. I pray that the eyes of your heart may be enlightened in order that you may know the hope to which he has called you, the riches of his glorious inheritance in his holy people, and his incomparably great power for us who believe. . . . I pray that out of his glorious riches he may strengthen you with power through his Spirit in your inner being, so that Christ may dwell in your hearts through faith. And I pray that you, being rooted and established in love, may have power, together with all the Lord's holy people, to grasp how wide and long and high and deep is the love of Christ, and to know this love that surpasses knowledge—that you may be filled to the measure of all the fullness of God. Now to him who is able to do immeasurably more than all we ask or imagine, according to his power that is at work within us, to him be glory in the church and in Christ Jesus throughout all generations, for ever and ever! Amen.

Ephesians 1:17–19a, 3:16–21

And now, so you can pray it for yourself, the same prayer, reworked.

God, give me your Spirit of wisdom and revelation.
  Help me know you better.
  Help the eyes of my heart be enlightened.
  Help me know the hope that you have called me to.
  Help me grasp the riches of your glorious inheritance.
  Help me trust that your incomparably great power is available to me.
  Help me believe.
  God, out of your glorious riches, will you strengthen me in my inner being by the power of the Holy Spirit?
  God, give me strength in my inner being so that Christ might dwell in my heart through faith.
  God, give me faith.
  Root me in your love.
  Establish me in your love.

Give me power to grasp how wide and long and high and deep the love of Christ is for me!
Help me grasp this love that is beyond knowledge.
Fill me up with all the fullness of yourself.
I believe that you are able to do far more than I can ask or imagine.
Your power is at work in me.
May you be glorified forever.
Amen.

Apply the TRUTH

- List out the specific negative thoughts you believe that tell you you are unaccepted or unwanted. Now list out the specific ways that Christ has made you acceptable.

- If you discover any sins you need to ask forgiveness for, ask God to forgive you on the basis of what Jesus has done to make you acceptable. And if you are carrying any guilt or shame about past sins, ask God to help you not hold against yourself anything he doesn't hold against you.

- In what ways do you try to earn God's acceptance? Try reciting Ephesians 2:8 whenever you catch yourself in that mindset.

- Look back at that list of true statements from Ephesians 2. Which of those truths about who you are in Christ most speaks to you? Why?

- Who could you share the light of Jesus with in your life in the coming weeks? Pray that God would give you an opportunity to do so.

- Print out the coloring sheet for Ephesians 2:8. As you color, practice reciting your verse.

Don't forget to get those bonus resources here!

FIIBGYHBSTF
ATINFYIITGOG
E2.8

FOR IT IS BY GRACE
YOU HAVE BEEN SAVED,
THROUGH FAITH—
AND THIS IS NOT
FROM YOURSELVES,
IT IS THE GIFT OF GOD.
EPHESIANS 2:8

TRUTH

FOR ANY TROUBLE

cayaoh
bhcfy

IP5.7

CAST ALL YOUR ANXIETY ON HIM
BECAUSE HE CARES FOR YOU.
I PETER 5:7

6

TRUTH When You're ANXIOUS

VERA

Cast all your anxiety on him because he cares for you.
—1 Peter 5:7

The Reality of Anxiety

I have always loved to compete.

From the time I was a little girl, I would lie in my bed the night before every gymnastics meet, visualizing my routines and dreaming about getting perfect tens on every event. My belly would flutter full of butterflies, and my heart would race a little bit as I went through every motion and movement of each of my routines. In the morning, my mom would pull my hair into two tightly braided pigtails, and I'd have trouble eating because of that pit in my stomach from all my nerves. The butterflies fluttered throughout the day, but once the meet was over, the jitters subsided, and I was back to being a little kid without a worry in the world.

Fast-forward a few years.

I traded in my pigtails and tumbling routines for pole vault-ing. It was a perfect fit: sprinting plus a little bit of gymnastics! I was *obsessed*, and I wanted to be the very best. I did all the work Rocky Balboa style—always doing one more rep. And it paid off. I won three state championships in high school and ended up earning myself a scholarship to Indiana University. In my time at IU, I worked my way to All-American honors and eventually trained for the 2016 USA Olympic team. I still got those nervous feelings of competition, but the butterflies were a bit different now, like they'd somehow grown and multiplied. And they didn't just accompany my meet day prep. I felt them way more often, more intensely, and for longer periods of time. In that last year going into the Olympic training, not always, but a lot of the time, I would feel anxious—especially when training and competitions weren't going well. I felt pressure to perform, fear of failing, and I worried a lot that the thing I'd spent so much time pouring myself into wasn't going to work out for me. It wasn't an *all-the-time* kind of feeling, but I would say I was generally anxious.

Fast-forward just a little more.

In 2016 I competed in my very last track meet ever. I finished seventeenth at the US Olympic team trials, and the one singular goal I had trained my whole life for was over. It was a heckuvah ride, and I am super proud of how I finished my career. But what was next? I had no idea how hard this next season of life was going to be. My whole life had been focused around this one singular goal, and now it was all over. Even though I knew my identity was in Jesus, even though I knew he had plans for me, even though I had the support of my loved ones . . . even though all of these things were true, I found myself slipping into a dark pit. For the next year I struggled with hardcore anxiety. Sometimes it was even difficult to wake up in the morning. I had a rough time leav-ing the house. Situations that weren't a big deal felt like a *huge* deal. It seemed that those butterflies had turned into bats, and they'd made their eternal home in the bottom of my belly. I felt sick, my heart raced, and I didn't know what to do about it. This was anxiety on a whole different level. Crippling anxiety. Even thinking about anxiety gave me anxiety.

cayaoh
bhcfy

IP5.7

I'm telling you all of this because I am no stranger to anxiety.

On one end of the spectrum there's the general situational anxiety that we've all felt at one time or another. Maybe it's having a bit of nerves about speaking in public or feeling a bit jittery about your first day at a new job. This situational anxiety swoops in for a moment, but once the event is over, it flies away. On the other end of the spectrum is crushing, persistent anxiety—anxiety that steals your joy, your focus, and your ability to thrive. Situations come and go, but the adrenaline and the nerves stay and even fray. Little things feel like big things, and your mind, spirit, and body pay the price.

For me, the overwhelming anxiety I faced after the 2016 Olympic trials was not just a downward spiral, but to make matters worse, my anxiety was wrapped up in shame. I was ashamed that I had anxiety, embarrassed even! I didn't want anyone to know. And because of that, I endured one of the hardest seasons of my life almost completely alone. I am putting this right here at the beginning of this chapter, because if that is you, I want to link arms with you right now and tell you that if you are alone in your head with your anxious thoughts, you don't have to stay alone. In this chapter, we are going to talk about filling our heads with the truth we need in order to war against our anxious thoughts, and I want you to do that with us!

But before we dive into God's truth, *hear this*: you aren't the only one struggling (19 percent of US adults struggle with anxiety disorders each year[1]), *and* you are not meant to fight your anxiety alone. Please, reach out for help. If this is something that you are struggling with, tell someone what is *really* going on in your heart—someone who will pray for you and walk with you through this time—a trusted friend, your pastor, your mentor, your mom, or a professional Christian counselor. If you are in an ongoing pattern of anxiety, if a cloud of sadness lingers over your life without lifting, or if you are in a depression that is so dark you can't see, please, friend, see a trained professional. There is no shame in seeking help. Isn't it the very thing you would advise your loved one to do? If I could go back in time and talk to my 2016 self, the one thing I would tell myself would be to tell someone sooner!

I want to say one more thing before we really get going.

If you are here, then you most likely live somewhere in the middle of that spectrum between butterflies and bats. I want you to lean in here, because it's important: whatever you're anxious about, it's real. Don't feel dumb or ashamed because other people don't deal with the thing you're dealing with in the same way you're dealing with it. If anyone has ever told you, "That's not that big of a deal! Don't be anxious about that!" and you've felt like an idiot, then let me say this to you: if it is making you anxious, then it is making you anxious! And no one here is judging your anxiety. Here is the good news: no threat, perceived or real, has to continue to have control over us! We are going to fight!

> **Whatever you're anxious about, it's real. Don't feel dumb or ashamed because other people don't deal with the thing you're dealing with in the same way you're dealing with it.**

So, let's lay down our shame for being anxious about big and little things.

Let's lay down our weariness from trying to fix the situations that are making us anxious.

Let's lay down our frustration about not being able to stop the anxiety in our own power.

Let's lay down the guilt we have for the unhealthy choices we've made in the middle of our anxious moments.

God loves us, and he has good things for us. Amen? We can trust him with our anxiety!

Truth to Overcome Anxiety

"Cast all your anxiety on him because he cares for you" (1 Peter 5:7). Now, you might look at our verse and think to yourself, *Ya think I haven't tried that one before?* This verse standing on its own might seem like the same flippant response that a friend might say to you when they're trying to be helpful: "Vera, just give your anxious thoughts to God." But as we dive into this verse and the surrounding passages, we'll unpack deep riches and otherworldly peace. What we want is a magic wand to wave over our anxiety and make it all go away, but what we will get is a deep understanding of God in the midst of our right now.

Our verse comes in the middle of a letter written by Peter, one of Jesus's main dudes. In fact, Jesus told Peter he would be the rock on which the church was built. Peter is writing this letter to encourage the church, the followers of Jesus throughout the world. In this chapter, I just want you to know that I'm going to be referencing all different parts of his letter to help us understand the bigger picture of what Peter was saying. If you have time, right now would be a great time to just take fifteen minutes and read that letter called 1 Peter. If you don't have a Bible handy, you can Google it; we use the NIV translation. Even though our verse doesn't come until chapter 5, I want to start our discussion with how Peter starts off his letter:

> Praise be to the God and Father of our Lord Jesus Christ! In his great mercy he has given us new birth into a living hope through

the resurrection of Jesus Christ from the dead, and into an in-heritance that can never perish, spoil or fade. This inheritance is kept in heaven for you, who through faith are shielded by God's power until the coming of the salvation that is ready to be revealed in the last time. In all this you greatly rejoice, though now for a little while you may have had to suffer grief in all kinds of trials. These have come so that the proven genuineness of your faith—of greater worth than gold, which perishes even though refined by fire—may result in praise, glory and honor when Jesus Christ is revealed.

1 Peter 1:3–7

Y'all, we could just close this book right now and bask in that glorious passage for a good long time, am I right? If that's you right now, go on ahead. For the rest of us, stick around as we unpack this passage together. I want you to see that before Peter teaches them anything at all, and well before we get to our verse, he reminds them of *this* foundational truth: because Jesus has conquered death itself, we can have a *living* (not dead) hope for a *new* life that's no longer riddled by our old self's struggles (like our sin and this fallen world and the resulting anxiety it brings us). As followers of Jesus, we have a *living* hope for heaven, where struggle and sin and suffering (*and* anxiety) are completely eliminated. But while we're still living in the struggles of this world, we can keep the faith because God will shield us by his power. And in the end, though we've endured all kinds of trials (like anxiety), we will have a strong faith! And what's more? We will get to share in the praise, glory, and honor of God!

Yes, yes, yes!

Peter *knew* that followers of Jesus needed to first and foremost be reminded of the reality of their situation in light of Jesus and what he has done! Surely his friends still struggled, surely they *were* anxious. Otherwise, why would our verse even be in this letter? And surely they would continue to struggle with the same sorts of things as long as they drew breath. But in the midst of their struggle and their anxiety, Peter reminds them of the truth of Jesus and the reality of his victory for all time. So, when we're facing something hard, like trying to overcome our anxious thoughts, we need to be reminded of the *living* hope that Jesus was raised from the dead! He conquered every hard thing when he conquered the grave. If Jesus was raised from the dead, anything is possible. Even being freed of our anxiety!

Anxiety is hard.

Jesus was raised from the dead.

Amen!

Let's Live This Out!

"Cast all your anxiety on him because he cares for you" (1 Peter 5:7). I can't tell you how eager I am to live out our verse! I want to cast my anxieties at the feet of Jesus. I want to believe that he cares for me. And I know you want to believe that too! But there are these negative thoughts, lies really, that we're believing that keep us from doing so. We might *know* in our minds that God is in control, but our practical response is anxiety. Our hearts still race with worry, telling us that our mind is wrong. In order to fight our anxious thoughts with God's truth, we must first see what the root of that anxiety is. There are three basic types of lies that cause our anxiety; let's take a look.

The Lie We Believe: My Situation Is in Control

Throughout his letter, Peter addresses the struggles his friends have been facing. These are the very things that are giving them anxiety, the things Peter is encouraging them to give to God. And if we flip back just one chapter before our verse, we see him address the stark reality of their struggle. Peter's friends are facing persecution, trials, and all sorts of suffering, and he draws attention to the temptation we all have to elevate our struggles above God.

> Dear friends, do not be surprised at the fiery ordeal that has come on you to test you, as though something strange were happening to you. But rejoice inasmuch as you participate in the sufferings of Christ, so that you may be overjoyed when his glory is revealed.
>
> 1 Peter 4:12–13

It's no secret that life is hard! Yet I often look at my own "fiery ordeal," and I am bewildered! Sometimes it feels like life is happening *to me*, that my situation is master over me, and I am subject to its bidding. Have you been there before? It's during times like this that we are tempted to think:

- *If only my situation were different, then I wouldn't be anxious anymore.*
- *If only I had more money, then I wouldn't be anxious anymore.*
- *If only I had a clean bill of health, then I wouldn't be anxious anymore.*
- *If only my kids were on the right path, then I wouldn't be anxious anymore.*
- *If only I were married, then I wouldn't be anxious anymore.*
- *If only I were more successful at work, then I wouldn't be anxious anymore.*

It feels like our situation is just too much for us. It's overwhelming and impossible. There's nothing we can do. Our situation is in control. It is *the* thing, *the* focus; we see it above and before everything else, even God.

The Truth: God Is in Control of My Situation

I'll say it again. *God* is in control. *Not* my situation, *not* yours. It might feel like our situations are in control because they are right up in our grills. We wake up to them in the morning. They persist through the night. They never stop happening to us. Notice that Peter says, "Dear friends, do not be surprised at the fiery ordeal that has come on you to test you, as though something strange were happening to you" (1 Peter 4:12). We may be surprised at the hardships in our life, but you know who isn't? God. He isn't surprised at all. He knows. He sees. And he has a plan. The next verse tells us that suffering is not the end of his plan for those who suffer according to his will. Again, Peter reminds us of the living hope we have in Jesus, that he will return, and that we will "be overjoyed when his glory is revealed" (v. 13). There is more going on than what we can see in our little corner of the world at this specific time. God knows all and sees all for all time. He has a plan, and he is God, so we can trust that he will execute it. Our God is not detached or unaware of our struggles. This is why Peter can tell his friends (and us) in 1 Peter 5:7 to "cast all your anxiety on him because he cares for you."

The Lie We Believe: I Am in Control

Another lie we tend toward (me especially) is that everything is up to me. We believe, *I am in control, and I am the one holding everything together.* Or we believe, *I am out of control, and it is all falling apart because of me.* Either way, everything is up to me. I am the single point of failure or success. If we look at the context of our verse, we see that in this passage, Peter is writing to the elders of the church, the leaders who *had* been entrusted with the responsibility of caring for God's people. He says to them, "Be shepherds of God's flock that is under your care, watching over them . . ." (1 Peter 5:2).

What I notice when I read this verse is that God entrusts very important, precious things to our care. For the elders, it is his own people. For us, it is every good thing we have:

Our children
Our friendships
Our spouse
Our finances
Our work
Our gifts, goals, and passions
Our home
Our community
Our body

What a gift that God gives us good and beautiful things to care for! Yet, our tendency is to take these wonderful things God has entrusted us with, and instead of caring for them, we start to believe that they are *our* things and that we are in control of them. We feel responsible for how they should or might go. We control them in the present moment, and we obsess about what the future holds for them. I know that for me, I continually try to control the things on that list. When those things are going well, I can have anxiety about keeping them going well. And when they aren't going well, I have anxiety about the fact that they are failing. I cause myself anxiety because I believe that it all depends on me (whether I realize it or not). I believe I am the one who is in control. I've put myself on the throne.

The Truth: God Is in Control of Me

Starting to see a pattern here yet? *God is in control.* He's not just in control of my situations, but he's in control of everything he's given me to oversee, *including me*! This means that when we're tempted to think it all depends on us, we can trust that it does not. Here is your takeaway: you are not the single point of success or failure. It's true that God entrusts us with responsibilities, even the care for his people. But we are not ultimately in charge of any of it. Just two verses after he calls the elders "shepherds" he says this: "And when the Chief Shepherd appears, you will receive the crown of glory that will never fade away" (1 Peter 5:4).

Do you see that? They may be shepherds, but they aren't the Chief Shepherd—Jesus is. They're merely undershepherds. They are not the boss of all of it, not ultimately responsible for the sheep. And this is true for us as well. Jesus may give us some really important responsibilities, but the buck doesn't stop with us, it stops with him. So all of those things we are tempted to fret about, they are all held in *his* competent hands, not ours. Moreover, just like we discussed earlier, our hope is a living hope, a hope that Jesus the Chief Shepherd is coming back. And when he does, he will give us a crown of glory, one that will never fade, one he earned for us with his perfect life.

Jesus may give us some really important responsibilities, but the buck doesn't stop with us, it stops with him. So all of those things we are tempted to fret about, they are all held in *his* competent hands, not ours.

Peter goes on to say that we can and should be humble "under God's mighty hand" (1 Peter 5:6). There's a twofold truth here for us that both humbles our pride and elevates our lowliness. On the one hand, God is the one who is mighty, not us. It doesn't depend on us. So, if we are prideful and have the tendency to think it all depends on us, he says to be humble. If instead we feel incapable, like we can't do it, Peter reminds us that God is mighty, and our strength is in him! This is good news for us no matter which spot we find ourselves in! He is the one who is in control—it depends on our mighty God!

What freedom this is! When those negative, anxious thoughts plague you, here are some true things you can tell yourself:

- Everything I have is God's!
- I take care of these things, steward them well, pray about them, and pay special attention to them, but they do not rest on my shoulders.
- I am not in control; God is.
- The success or failure of things does not ultimately depend on me.
- I'm an undershepherd; God is the Chief Shepherd.
- Because God is mighty, I don't have to be.
- I can give my anxiety to God, because he is in control of all the things that make me anxious, and he is good.

The Lie We Believe: The Enemy Is in Control

We are up against an enemy. And he is a liar, a thief, and a murderer. He is a very real threat. And even if we *know* that God is over him, we often live like the enemy has the ultimate power in our life. Satan is up against us, and it feels like he's winning.

Peter describes Satan as big, powerful, hungry, and angry. He says, "Your enemy the devil prowls around like a roaring lion looking for someone to devour" (1 Peter 5:8). He is a lion ready to devour us. He is scheming, whispering in our ears that he is the one over us and our hard situations. We give  him power in our life to make us anxious and defeated. We believe that he's the one who is mighty, powerful, and in control.

In 2016, in my lowest of lows, when I was alone and in my own head, there were moments when I'd given Satan a real foothold. His lies were loud, my anxiety was crippling, and I lived like he was all powerful. It sure felt like the enemy was in control.

The Truth: God Is in Control of the Enemy

Friend, that old enemy, the snake, the serpent, the deceiver, the murderer, the roaring lion, he is real. He is powerful. But he is not all powerful.

God is.

And God is in control.

Let's finish the rest of those verses about our enemy.

> Be alert and of sober mind. Your enemy the devil prowls around like a roaring lion looking for someone to devour. Resist him, standing firm in the faith, because you know that the family of believers throughout the world is undergoing the same kind of sufferings. And the God of all grace, who called you to his eternal glory in Christ, after you have suffered a little while, will himself restore you and make you strong, firm and steadfast. To him be the power for ever and ever. Amen.
>
> 1 Peter 5:8–11

Who is the one in control? Who is victorious? God, who has the power for ever and ever. God—the God of all grace who calls you and me into eternal glory! God, who himself will restore us and make us strong and firm and steadfast. And God, who is in control of all things and is victorious, has called us to share in his victory over the devil. Our job in all of this: to be sober and aware of our enemy and to stand firm and resist him in the strength and courage that God provides. We can do this, not by our power but by God's! By his power, we can stand against the enemy and are promised victory! Here are just a few other things the Bible tells us about this:

God will crush Satan under our feet (see Romans 16:20).

Jesus has given us authority over all the power of the enemy (see Luke 10:19).

God disarmed and triumphed over the enemy by the cross (see Colossians 2:15).

God has given us armor to resist the enemy's schemes (see Ephesians 6:11).

God is on the throne over everything in heaven and on earth; we just have to remember it, believe it, and allow him back on the throne of our own lives. What good news! We can silence the lion's roar and send him running by the power God gives us. We can rest our anxious hearts in God's victory over our enemy.

So, Now What?

We do the thing. We become alert and sober minded by putting God's Word in our mind and heart. I don't know if it is just me, but our truth has become more beautiful, full, and grand than it seemed at first glance: "Cast all your anxiety on him because he cares for you" (1 Peter 5:7).

We follow a big, caring, powerful, victorious, personal God. He is bigger than our situation. He is bigger than us. He is bigger than our enemy. And he is in control. He cares for us. And we can trust him with our anxious thoughts.

When we lean into his care, we receive these promises in return:

He restores us.
He strengthens us.
He makes us firm.
He makes us steadfast.

Pain, suffering, and stress will keep coming. But we will not be the same. We will be stronger and able to endure. These memory verses are gifts for every new situation that threatens to cause our hearts to race and our minds to swirl. We will not be surprised.

We will stand firm. We will resist the enemy. And we will cast our anxiety on God because he cares for us!

As I look back on my darkest season of anxiety, I look with tender sadness and rejoicing. I have truly experienced God's presence with me in my suffering. My love for and reliance on God's Word came from that time, and it's out of that suffering that Dwell was born. I made my mind alert by memorizing and meditating on God's Word day and night. In the middle of it, I couldn't see how this suffering would ever be used for good. But I trusted him. And he was so kind and gentle to me as I walked through the valley. And now, I can say with all confidence, I rejoice for my suffering! To him be the power for ever and ever. Amen!

─────────── Apply the TRUTH ───────────

- What specific anxious thoughts tend to get stuck in your negative thought loop?
- Do you believe that everything depends on you? And how does that add to your anxiety?
- What is one practical way you can remember that God is in control of your situation when you start to feel anxious?
- How is it a relief to know that God is in control of all the things, including you?
- How do you believe the lie that the enemy is in control?
- What did you read in this chapter that helps you understand the victory you have over Satan?
- Make a list of all the things that make you anxious. Then write at the top of your list "God is in control of" and pray through your list, giving all your anxiety to God.
- Who can you share your struggle with? A friend, a pastor, a counselor?

Did you listen to the podcast episode for this verse yet? Listen in to hear more about how Natalie and I have found so much freedom from anxiety by memorizing God's truth.

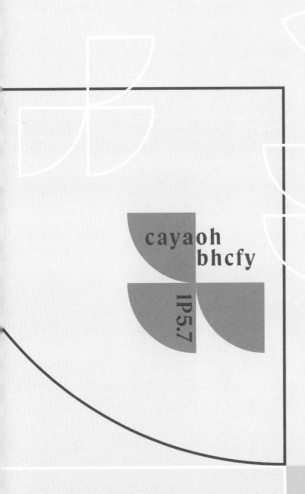

cayaoh
bhcfy

1P5.7

CAST ALL YOUR ANXIETY ON HIM
BECAUSE HE CARES FOR YOU.
I PETER 5:7

WHY,
MY SOUL,
ARE YOU
DOWNCAST?
WHY SO
DISTURBED
WITHIN
ME?
PUT YOUR
HOPE
IN GOD,
FOR I
WILL YET
PRAISE
HIM,
MY SAVIOR
AND
MY GOD.
PSALM 42:5

wmsaydwsdwmpyhigfiwyphmSamG

P42.5

7

TRUTH When You're DEPRESSED

NATALIE

Why, my soul, are you downcast? Why so disturbed within me? Put your hope in God, for I will yet praise him, my Savior and my God.

—Psalm 42:5

Dark Valleys

If life is a journey, then the one place we fear to tread and try to avoid is the dark valley. And yet, often our paths veer into these deep valleys. There was a time when I went through such a deep, dark valley that I was more than depressed; I was disturbed, I was distraught. In 2019, we moved our big fat family of seven from small, sweet Hershey, Pennsylvania, to big, exciting, urban Chicago (based on that date, I'm sure you know where this is headed, right?). Well, we gave up the known goodness of our situation to move closer to family and to answer God's call to minister in the city.

We were excited for our new adventure!

We were hopeful for all the new opportunities, expectant for a new community and a new church family—a new place where our people could thrive. But of course, our hopes were snuffed out by COVID. Just months after our transition, the world shut down, and we were shut up in our small condo, doing life and work and school by ourselves online day after endless day, month after miserable month. I watched my family slowly wither, my once-bright children darken and withdraw, without friends or even the possibility of friends. All our excitement and hopes were dashed, and any small, reasonable anxieties we'd had about our move were magnified and realized. What was supposed to be a dream became a nightmare, one I couldn't wake from.

I'd like to tell you that I persevered, that my faith was strong and vibrant, that we sang songs of praise from our COVID prison, but if we had a song at all, it was a lament. I felt hopelessness in a way I never had before. I saw my people suffering and felt completely helpless to do anything about it. Each day became a battle for hope and joy.

I needed words to fight the gloom.

But I had none. As the dark cloud settled over our home, I didn't know how to express my sadness. I am a word person. I have all the words. All the time. Yet, I couldn't frame my thoughts, and my feelings were so dark and disturbed that they startled me. It was as if I'd forgotten everything—the truth I knew from Scripture was overshadowed by my situation. I would try to pray but found I couldn't.

I needed words, words I didn't have. So, I turned to God's book to find any words that would resonate with my feelings. And there I found words—words of other people caught in a dark valley, crying out to God for light—the words I desperately needed to give utterance to my own despairing heart. Psalm 42 was one such place. Those words became my words! The

psalmist's confusion was my confusion, his complaint, my complaint,
his doubt, my doubt. And slowly,
his hope became my hope, his remembrance of goodness, my remembrance, his fragile faith, my faith. His

honest refrain (our verse) became my
refrain: "Why, my soul, are you downcast?
Why so disturbed within me? Put your hope in God, for I will
yet praise him, my Savior and my God" (Psalm 42:5).

If this is you right now, you are welcome here.

If you feel lost and desperate, alone in the dark with no fore-
seeable way out, I'm truly sorry. I've been there, and I know how
helpless it can feel. Know this: your sadness is welcome here.
Your wordlessness, your hopelessness, your doubt and confusion,
your struggle and your pain, your anger and your complaints, they
are all welcome here. All your negative thoughts and feelings are
welcome right here, right now.

This is the place for them. This is the place for you to be honest
and real, to walk the path through the dark valley of this psalm.
You can know this is the right place for you, because this psalm is
in Scripture, and this psalmist is right where you are, struggling
through the seemingly endless bog, wondering, *Where are you,
God? Why me? How did I get here?* May his words give you words—
honest words for your feelings, for your doubts and fears, words
of despair and longing, but also words of hope, words of remembrance of God and his goodness, words to carry you through this
dark valley and out into the light again.

If this isn't you right now, you're welcome too.

I'm gonna bet that if this isn't you right now, you can at least
relate. You've been through that dark valley before. And the
truth is, you know you will again. So, this is still for you, maybe
not for now, but sadly and surely for later. Let this walk through
the dark valley be a place of learning. There are principles and

lessons here for all of us—to equip us for our future struggles. I am convinced that once you walk through Psalm 42, you will come back again and again, until this chapter in your Bible becomes an old dog-eared friend just like it is in mine. Let's read it now.

Psalm 42
For the director of music. A *maskil* of the Sons of Korah.

1 As the deer pants for streams of water,
so my soul pants for you, my God.
2 My soul thirsts for God, for the living God.
When can I go and meet with God?
3 My tears have been my food
day and night,
while people say to me all day long,
"Where is your God?"
4 These things I remember
as I pour out my soul:
how I used to go to the house of God
under the protection of the Mighty One
with shouts of joy and praise
among the festive throng.

5 Why, my soul, are you downcast?
Why so disturbed within me?
Put your hope in God,
for I will yet praise him,
my Savior and my God.

6 My soul is downcast within me;
therefore I will remember you
from the land of the Jordan,
the heights of Hermon—from Mount Mizar.
7 Deep calls to deep

---

in the roar of your waterfalls;
all your waves and breakers
have swept over me.

8 By day the LORD directs his love,
at night his song is with me—
a prayer to the God of my life.

9 I say to God my Rock,
"Why have you forgotten me?
Why must I go about mourning,
oppressed by the enemy?"
10 My bones suffer mortal agony
as my foes taunt me,
saying to me all day long,
"Where is your God?"

11 Why, my soul, are you downcast?
Why so disturbed within me?
Put your hope in God,
for I will yet praise him,
my Savior and my God.

Isn't this beautiful and vulnerable and heartbreaking? Now, I want you to go back and read it again, read it slowly and consider it, even get a pencil out and mark it up.

Answer these questions:

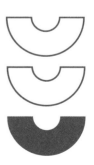

- What's the main point?
- What words and phrases are repeated?
- Who's the psalmist talking to?
- What stands out to you?
- How does the psalmist feel, and what does the psalmist do with his feelings?

Six Takeaways from Psalm 42

I hope you saw some of the honest struggle and the profound hope in this psalm! It's a model for us of what we should do when we're downcast, disturbed, and depressed. There's a lot here, more than we can cover. But I'm going to highlight for you six ways this psalm informs how we should think about and respond in our own low valleys.

1. Stop Feeling Bad about Feeling Bad

Right here, right out of the blocks, I want to dispel any lie you've ever been told (by others or yourself or the enemy) that depression is due to your lack of faith or that real, strong Christians don't struggle with depression because they have the joy and hope of Christ. Depression is a reality for many faithful Christians. As a pastor's wife, I've counseled too many people struggling under the burden of deep sadness only to discover that their burden is twice as heavy because of the deep shame they feel for feeling depressed. So let me expose that lie right here and now with this psalm.

Do you see who's struggling with honest hopelessness and despair here? A real live author of the Bible! A "son of Korah," one of the psalmists, who has penned for posterity his own deep depression, despair, and doubt for all to read! Why would this be here, if not for us? His honest struggle for hope is a model for us! And he is not the lone example in the pages of God's book. There are countless stories of so many others—anointed kings, prophets, priests, apostles, and other psalmists—all who struggled against despair. The struggle is real, and real believers struggle. Let's not pile shame on top of suffering.

Friend, I want you to hear this right now: Jesus is not disappointed with you because you are sad. He isn't condemning you for your lack of faith. He knows your burden fully, and he wants to bear it *with* you. He says, "Come to me, all you who are weary and burdened, and I will give you rest" (Matthew 11:28). Would you let him carry it? Would you rest in him? He is calling to you in that deep valley, asking you to stop hiding from him in shame, so that he can take your burden and walk *with* you through the darkness.

> **Jesus is not disappointed with you because you are sad. He isn't condemning you for your lack of faith. He knows your burden fully, and he wants to bear it *with* you.**

2. You Are Not Meant to Suffer in Silence All Alone

Before we dive into the deep end of this poor psalmist's suffering, I just want to take note of the subtitle of this psalm. It says that it's "for the director of music." This may not have hit you—in fact, you might have even skimmed over it—but this song is meant to be sung *with others*. The Psalms aren't just a beautiful, heartfelt collection of poetry but the hymnal of the church! While this particular song is a deeply personal confession, it's also meant to be sung with others. There is comfort here. The collective people of God are called to weep together, to cry out in honest confession, "My soul thirsts for God" and "Why are you downcast?" *together*! In fact, you'll notice that one of the things the psalmist most misses is worshiping with the people of God (v. 4). Collective suffering is implicit in this corporate song!

So hear me say this to you: do not weep alone.

You are not called to suffer alone but to weep with others (Romans 12:15). When you find yourself in the dark valley, do not travel it alone. Your sadness is not all your own. You were not meant to bear the burden alone. Yes, Jesus bears it with you, but you should also allow others into your pain and suffering. I know you may feel bad about burdening someone with your problems, but let me assure you, they *want* to help you carry them. Here's how you can know they do: don't you want to help your friends carry their burdens? I thought so. And they want to do the same for you.

This is also the very thing God wants his people to do! We are called to "carry each other's burdens" (Galatians 6:2), to "weep with those who weep" (Romans 12:15 ESV), and to "lay down our lives for our brothers and sisters" just as Jesus laid his life down for us (1 John 3:16). So, stop trying to be strong on your own! Invite a trusted friend to cry with you, counsel you, pray for you, and follow up with you. You should also go to your pastor and elders, whose specific job is to keep watch over your soul (Hebrews 13:17). They can advise, help, and pray for you. And certainly, if you experience a longer season or more regular bouts of depression, seek a trained Christian counselor. They have more wisdom, specific experience, and expertise to help you through your struggle. You were never meant to bear the burden by yourself; it is too much for you. And if you're carrying a heavy burden all by yourself, let today be the day you stop carrying it alone.

3. Depression Is Confusing and Disconcerting

Did you notice as you read through this psalm that the psalmist is completely befuddled? He can't seem to figure out his feelings. The rational part of himself keeps addressing his soul (or his emotional self), trying to discover what the problem is and to encourage his soul. He keeps asking his soul questions like *Why are you downcast? Why are you disturbed? When will you feel close to God again?* He's legitimately dumbfounded by his feelings! He can't understand why they are the way they are!

Can I just get an "Amen!" here?!

This is my every experience of depression. It brings me great comfort to know that I'm not the only one who is completely caught off guard by depression. When I'm down, it's like my brain and my heart are totally disconnected. On the one hand, I know how I *should* feel, I know how I *want* to feel, and on the other hand, I somehow can't seem to make my feelings match up with what I know to be true. In my thinking brain, I know the truth, but in my feeling heart, I'm all tangled up. Like the psalmist, I find myself asking, "Why am I so depressed?" So here's my takeaway: it's normal when you go through these dark valleys to feel baffled by your feelings and wonder how you got there. Like we learned in chapter 4 of this book, "the heart is deceitful" and difficult to understand (Jeremiah 17:9). If you feel disconcerted and confused by your feelings, you can know that your feelings aren't always in line with what you know in your head to be true. That's why it's so important for us to speak truth back to ourselves when we know our feelings aren't matching up with what we believe in our heads.

4. You Can Be Real about How You Feel

This is no candy-coated, cleaned-up psalm. It's the real, raw admission of a seriously distraught human. The psalmist "pour[s] out [his] soul" (v. 4). He confesses that he cries all day and night (v. 3). People are telling him that God's abandoned him (vv. 3, 10). He feels like he's drowning (v. 7). He doubts if God is there (v. 9). And he feels like he's gonna die (v. 10). His situation feels dire, and he's completely frank about how he feels about it. He shares all his negative thoughts honestly—all his doubts and fears and struggles. He wonders, *Where is God?* And his emotions answer back, *Far away, far away. Does God even care? Does he see?* It has been too long since he felt God in his soul. Where is he? Why has God forgotten him? He is in the middle of the dark valley. And he's not mincing his words.

What does this tell us? Because the psalmist is completely candid with his every negative thought, then we can and even *should* be real with our negative thoughts too. When you are low, do as this psalmist does. Be honest with yourself, be honest with others, be honest with God—brutally honest. God, for one, can handle it.

You can say it all to him. If you feel like God has abandoned you, tell him! If you feel like you're drowning and everything is way too much, just say it. If you feel attacked on all sides, then cry out! Say it all. Get all those negative thoughts and feelings out, expose them, talk about them, lay them all out for what they are. Hiding your feelings won't make them go away or get better. If you are going to find healing, you have to start by acknowledging the hurt.

5. Fight Your Negative Thoughts and Feelings with Truth!

I love how the psalmist is brutally honest with what he's thinking and feeling. He knows he is not okay, and yet here's the thing: he isn't okay to stay that way. His thoughts and feelings disturb him, and he longs to feel differently. So, instead of wallowing, he preaches truth to his soul. He fights his negative thoughts and feelings with truth in three ways. And he gives us a model of what to do when we're reeling too.

■ Remember the Truth of Better Times

Instead of believing the accusers telling him that God has forgotten him, instead of withdrawing into his own fear that they must be right, the psalmist leans into his recollection of better times, the times when he felt near God. He reminds himself how he "used to go to the house of God under the protection of the Mighty One with shouts of joy and praise among the festive throng" (Psalm 42:4). What a thing to tell your soul to do in the middle of depression! "Remember your joy! Remember how it felt to celebrate and feast as you worshiped God with his people!" This is his response to the threatening darkness: "Remember the light! The darkness isn't all there is." He reminds himself of the good times he's known in order to encourage his soul to believe that they will come again.

Have you ever done this? In a dark season, have you ever looked back at the good old days and let them buoy your soul? I for sure have. I have pulled out old photo albums. I have read old letters. I have closed my eyes and sat in the sun, imagining times in the mountains. I have written out lists of how I've seen God show up in my life. I have called old friends and caught up. These remembrances really did give me hope through the dark valley that there would be a sunny day on the mountaintop to come.

■ Remind Yourself of This Truth: God Is in Control

The psalmist recognizes a good but difficult truth in the midst of his lament—God is in control of his suffering. When he points out that he's drowning, notice how he says it: "Deep calls to deep in the roar of *your* waterfalls; all *your* waves and breakers have swept over me" (Psalm 42:7, emphasis added). He acknowledges that God is in control of everything, even his suffering. And yet, instead of deepening his despair, this fact gives him hope. In the very next verse, he says, "By day the LORD directs his love, at night his song is with me—a prayer to the God of my life" (Psalm 42:8). Isn't this the most beautiful image? In the midst of his incomprehensible difficulties, he clings to God. He calls God "the God of my life"—the one he prays to and sings to in the middle of his dark night. This is what he knows: God sees me. God loves me. God is in control. Because God loves him, because God is in control even of his suffering, he can have solace knowing that God will see him through this suffering.

I know it might not feel very comforting that God is in control of your suffering, but I assure you, you do not want the opposite. You do not want your pain and suffering to be outside his authority. You do not want the dark valley to be random and purposeless. You don't want a God who is caught off guard by the suffering you experience in this broken world. Rather, you want a God who works all things together for the good of his children—even (and most especially) our suffering (Romans 8:28). You want a good God who not only knows the end of the story but who, by his boundless power, will bring about an absolutely good ending—one where he wipes our every tear, ends all our suffering, and ushers in a perfect eternity with him. We need God to be in control of our suffering. We can trust that he is good, he loves us, and he will one day bring us out of the dark valley for all time.

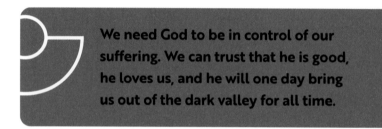

We need God to be in control of our suffering. We can trust that he is good, he loves us, and he will one day bring us out of the dark valley for all time.

■ Repeat the Truth

We need the truth on repeat to fight our negative thoughts and feelings. Twice, the psalmist asks his emotional self, "Why, my soul, are you downcast? Why so disturbed within me?" And both times he answers with this: "Put your hope in God, for I will yet praise him, my Savior and my God" (Psalm 42:5, 11). When his soul is despairing and disturbed, he tells himself instead to hope in God. He reminds himself that this isn't the end of all things. He will again praise God, his Savior, the one who will rescue him out of his dark valley. I love that he repeats the exact same words to himself, just like we do when we memorize verses. His depression is persistent, and so his response is consistent. He keeps on responding with the same repetitive truth.

Okay, I just have to say it. This psalmist is modeling exactly what we want you to do in this book: preach truth to yourself! When things are all good, and especially when they are not, your soul needs God's truth. When your heart tells you to despair, you can respond, "Put your hope in God, for I will yet praise him, my Savior and my God" (vv. 5, 11). When your fear says God has abandoned you, remind yourself, "By day the LORD directs his love, at night his song is with me—a prayer to the God of my life" (v. 8). God's truth is bigger than your feelings, more positive than your negative thoughts, more powerful than your sadness, more hopeful than your despair. Let it be so. May you experience this truth in your deep valley: God is with you, God cares, God is in control, and you can trust in him! Remind your heart that you have a Savior who loves you and who walks with you through your dark valley. He has not abandoned you, no matter how much it might feel like he has. His love is there, whether you feel it or not. So like our friend the psalmist, keep God's truths on repeat in your mind to overcome your negative thoughts and feelings.

6. Even When There Isn't Resolution, There Is Hope

I want you to notice something about this psalm: there is no resolution. It doesn't start in the low valley and end high on the mountain. Nope, it ends, and the psalmist is still in the dark valley. It ends without resolution; it ends with the psalmist still fighting his feelings with the truth. The psalmist's problems are not abated, he still feels distant from God, and his rational self and his emotional self are not aligned. Our psalm ends with the refrain we find in the middle: "Why, my soul, are you downcast? Why so disturbed within me? Put your hope in God, for I will yet praise him, my Savior and my God" (Psalm 42:5, 11). He's still wondering why he's downcast and disturbed. He's still preaching hope to his soul. I know. This is not the ending you wanted, but I promise, this is the ending you need—it's the ending we all need! There is good news in this unresolved psalm. It's why I chose our verse in particular.

I chose our verse not because it's settled and final but because it's still stuck in the messy middle. Just. Like. Us. Nothing this side of heaven is ever fully resolved, finally good, completely right. We live our lives with unresolved sadness, here in the in-between. As long as we draw breath, we will struggle, we will always have reasons to drag our lagging heart along with the hope of Christ. We will always need to preach to our souls because we live in a broken world that constantly hurts us, and we are a sinful people who constantly wander from the truth. Our loose ends are never neatly tied up. And that is precisely why we need this messy, back-and-forth psalm with this unresolved verse of hope. When *we* are downcast, when *we* are disturbed, we can tell ourselves this truth: "Put your hope in God, for I will yet praise him, my Savior and my God" (v. 11). There is hope, hope that is still to come, hope in a God we call Savior, hope in a promise that we will one day realize.

Indeed we *will* yet praise God, and fully! One day, he will tie up every loose end. Our situations *will* get better, finally and perfectly. We will no longer have need for hope, because all our hopes will be met in Christ. But until that day, in this messy middle, we can look to our Savior and our God and praise him now. We can hold on to hope in the face of despair and depression. We can fight our feelings with the truth we know and believe.

--- **Apply the TRUTH** ---

- What keeps you from sharing your burdens with others?
- What keeps you from sharing your burdens with God?
- Have you ever felt ashamed for feeling depressed?
- How is it comforting to know that throughout the Bible people have been honest and vulnerable with their depression?
- If you're depressed, take time to get out all of your negative thoughts and feelings. Get out all your sadness,

everything that is confusing, all your despair, all your disappointment. Start by writing it down. Then, tell God. Tell a close friend. Tell your pastor or an elder at your church. Tell a counselor. You were not meant to carry this burden all by yourself.

- Have you ever looked back at the good old days and let them buoy your soul? Write out a list of some of the ways you've seen God's loving hand in your life.
- If you are not currently struggling, who do you know who is? How might you support them?
- Practice saying this verse on repeat, just like the psalmist did. Be sure to put the digital image on your phone to help you memorize the verse.

Pour It Out, All Your Soul
By Natalie Abbott

If day and night, you eat only tears,
And your soul thirsts for God, God alone,
If the taunt of abandonment rings in your ears,
And the doubt in your soul cries "he's gone,"
If the waves pull you down, in the breakers you drown,
If you feel forgotten, oppressed, near to death,
Let it out. Pour it out, all your soul.
Here and now, spread it out on the floor.
All your sadness, your questions, your doubts.
Air them out, pour it out, all your soul.

When you're done, all wrung out, empty and worn,
Only then, fill your soul with this truth, you still know:
You are seen, you are loved, you are known.
You feel lost in the dark, but you're never alone.
You've been full, you've drunk deep, you've known joy on your lips.
You've felt love, all day long, and your heart was a song.
Through the day, in the night, he was there, always there.
He feels far, but he's near, even now, even here.
O my soul, your pain isn't unknown. You are never alone.
You are seen, you are loved, you are known.

WHY,
MY SOUL,
ARE YOU
DOWNCAST?
WHY SO
DISTURBED
WITHIN
ME?
PUT YOUR
HOPE
IN GOD,
FOR I
WILL YET
PRAISE
HIM,
MY SAVIOR
AND
MY GOD.
PSALM 42:5

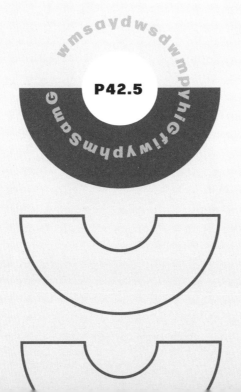

P42.5

HAVE I NOT
COMMANDED YOU?
BE STRONG AND COURAGEOUS.
DO NOT BE AFRAID;
DO NOT BE DISCOURAGED,
FOR THE LORD YOUR GOD
WILL BE WITH YOU
WHEREVER YOU GO.
JOSHUA 1:9

HINCY BSAC DNBA DNBD

FTLYGWBWYWYG J1.9

8

TRUTH When You're AFRAID

VERA

Have I not commanded you? Be strong and courageous. Do not be afraid; do not be discouraged, for the LORD your God will be with you wherever you go.

—Joshua 1:9

My Anthem

I recently got a text from my oldest brother, Curtis.

He sent me a screenshot of his Pandora playlist showing the song "For Those About to Rock (We Salute You)" by AC/DC. This is what his text read: "National Championships after the rain break. I think at Drake. Do you remember them playing this song? Every time I hear it, that is the moment I think of. I was only a spectator and I was ready to run through a wall when they started playing that song."

Do I remember? How could I forget?

In my senior year as a pole vaulter on the track and field team at Indiana University, my goal was to win the title of National

Champion. Coming off a Big Ten Championship title and new meet record, things were really lining up heading into the National Championship. Many of my siblings and their kiddos, as well as Matt (my now husband, then boyfriend) and another good friend all traveled to watch the meet. Having all my people there was everything.

This meet was mine to win.

I remember getting my pole, my run, and my jump all dialed in as we warmed up. I was in peak fitness, my legs had all the pop, I was fast, strong, and ready. As I finished my jumps, I put my sweats on and sat quietly listening to the chatter of my competitors. Many of them were worrying and complaining about the rain that was supposed to roll in. Some were discussing injuries that were nagging. One of them was arguing with their coach. I found myself thinking, *Half the field has already defeated themselves; now I just have to beat the other half.*

Here was my chance.

For those of you unfamiliar with pole vault, you get three chances to clear the bar. If you fail in those three attempts, you are out of the competition. If you clear, the bar is raised higher and you get three new attempts. Just after I cleared my second height, a nasty rainstorm started rolling in. The meet was put on delay, and all the athletes were ushered under the stadium to wait out the storm. I remember lying on my back, eyes closed, visualizing exactly what I wanted to happen, jump after jump, until I was the last one standing. After an hour or so the storm passed, and we made our way back out of the tunnel.

This was the moment.

There was steam rising up off the track as the water evaporated from the June-hot rubber. And as we walked single file toward the pole vault pit, a song started ringing out over the loudspeakers. The simple, repetitive guitar intro of "For Those About to Rock (We Salute You)" by AC/DC flooded my whole body with adrenaline. This song was one of my all-time training anthems! And as the drum beat in my soul, memories from my childhood flashed through my head—I'm in my basement alongside my oldest brother, Curtis, repping out pull-ups, maxing on the bench press, sit-ups upon sit-ups, handstand holds, running sprints up the big hill in front of our house . . . Now I'm racing up long sets of stairs to the top of a hill at my middle school until I almost puke . . . Now I'm in high school, training even harder to make state champ. My brother is right there by my side in every memory, encouraging me, pushing me, telling me I could do anything I set out to do. The music transported me back all those years to the times when I was training for and dreaming of *this very moment*. Now I was here, and the music pulsated through me—the locomotive beat of that song, the scream of the lead singer, Brian Johnson—there would be no beating me today. I believed with every fiber of my being that I was going to win. This was my day, my moment. Fearless. Confident. I would not be denied.

Courage pulsed through my body with that anthem.

That song was powerful enough to create in me a sense of strength that made me feel invincible. There had been times in my career when the fear of failing had gotten in my head. But not today. I was reminded of all I'd done to prepare for this moment, and I trusted I could do what I'd come to do. I did not fear anyone or anything. I did not consider failure. I would win.

We Need an Anthem!

Our verse for this chapter is like that song—an anthem of strength and courage louder and more urgent than any lurking fear. Hear the promise and power in it: "Have I not commanded you? Be strong and courageous. Do not be afraid; do not be discouraged, for the LORD your God will be with you wherever you go" (Joshua 1:9).

But before we learn to sing the words of this anthem verse, before we can find courage and strength in them, we need to understand first what we're up against.

What Are We So Afraid Of?

Not to trivialize my competition fears, but in this grown-up world we have a lot more to fear than not getting over the bar in three tries and winning the trophy. Here are just a few of the negative thoughts that spring rapidly to mind when it comes to fear:

We fear failure.
We fear what other people think of us.
We fear making a choice that turns out to be the wrong one.
We fear for the well-being of our loved ones.
We fear we might let those same loved ones down.
We fear our loved ones might let us down.
We fear people won't love us if we show our real self.
We fear rejection.
We fear abandonment.
We fear being alone.
We fear change.
We fear challenge.
We fear the world.
We fear war.
We fear that things have been too good, so bad things must be on the horizon.
We fear the unknown—what's going to happen?
We fear a diagnosis.
We fear suffering.

We fear the devil and his schemes against us.

We fear death.

This is in no way an exhaustive list, but I am certain of this: all of us have faced at least one of these at some point. And all of them are real. When I first became a mom, I regularly struggled with this negative thought: *my kids are going to die.* If they slept fifteen minutes longer than normal, I'd start getting antsy. So, I did what any new mom would do—stealthily slip into their room and place my finger just below their nostrils till I felt them breathe out. Sometimes I'd walk out and immediately think to myself, *Did I really feel breath? I'm not so sure now . . . maybe I'll just check one more time.*

Once those initial fears of keeping my little humans alive started to wane, my mind was filled with the fears of deeper stuff—of messing them up, of doing the whole parenting thing wrong. The constant choices about every last thing would send me spiraling— the endless *shoulds* and *should nevers*—you should only feed your kids this, you should never (*ever*) use that product on their skin, you should only ever put them to sleep this way at these times, you should never let them do x, y, z or it will ruin everything. It all seemed so intense! And then, in the next Google search, I'd receive the exact opposite advice from some other so-called expert. Surely, I was doing it all wrong! Parenting has the potential to crush and exhaust the most brave and confident person with the fear of failing.

Whatever the thing is that we're afraid of, whatever fearful thought plays on repeat in our minds, we must know this about fear: it is a relentless enemy. It can threaten us with the physical presence of anxiety in our bodies. Fear can become our captain, the driving force behind our decisions. Fear can be our jailer, keeping us locked up in our own world behind the bars of the worst possible scenario. Even for the strongest believer, fear can have very real power to paralyze us, leaving us totally uncertain. So what do we do? We are strong and take courage.

This Is No Trite Saying

"Have I not commanded you? Be strong and courageous. Do not be afraid; do not be discouraged, for the LORD your God will be with you wherever you go" (Joshua 1:9). It's an awesome verse, but if we aren't careful, it might sound like a middle school poster.

Do you remember those cheesy posters? You know the ones hanging in your math class with an inspiring image and some matching virtue below it? I can remember times of absolute boredom, staring for hours at one particular poster of skydivers in different colored outfits, holding hands, hundreds (thousands?) of feet above the ground, making some design with their bodies. And below the image it read *TEAMWORK*. Was there a middle school in America that didn't have that poster?

We don't want our verse on a middle school poster.

If we don't really understand our verse, it can easily start to sound like one of those posters. I feel like the right image for it would be a rock climber hanging off the edge of a cliff with a

sunset in the background and the word *COURAGE*. Does that poster have the power to inspire me to just dig down deep and not be afraid? *Yeah, right.* What was meant to inspire me feels cliché and deflating. It's nothing more than an empty directive lacking any power to give us the courage it tells us to have. We need so much more than a one-line pep talk. Why? Because we know, deep inside us, that we need help. We might be able to be "strong and courageous" in our own strength for a moment, a day, a season even, but we do not have the infinite resources it requires to remain steadfast, to stay strong, to be resilient, and to not give in to our fear. Our verse will fall flat if it's nothing more than a motivational mountain poster. So what should we do?

If this verse is going to be our anthem of courage in times of fear, then we must plunge into the depths of its words and context in order to unfold the source of its strength.

A Short History of God's Faithfulness

The verse we're looking at comes out of the book of Joshua. Even if you aren't the churchy type, you might know Joshua for being the guy who walked a bunch of people around a town called Jericho, and then they all yelled until the walls fell down. But way before this happened, God was building a story not about the strength and power and courage of Joshua or the people he was leading, but a story about himself—his power, his faithfulness, and his trustworthiness in times of need.

Let's Start Back at the Beginning

If we go back a bit, the story of Joshua begins in Egypt, where Joshua is a slave along with all the other people of God, the Israelites. In a mind-bending chain of events, God exerts his power over Pharaoh and the Egyptians through his leader, Moses, in order to bring about freedom for his people. He sends these wild plagues on the Egyptians and allows Moses to do wonders before Pharaoh, until finally, Pharaoh lets God's people go. The story ends with one of the most notable and awe-inspiring miracles of the whole Bible: the splitting of the Red Sea. After Pharaoh agrees to let the Israelites free, he goes back on his word and pursues them. God leads the people to the edge of the Red Sea, and by the time Pharaoh catches up to them, the Israelites are cornered. On one side is an impassable body of water, and on the other side, Pharaoh's army. The people are facing certain death. All is lost. Then God commands Moses to stretch his hands over the water, and God splits the water and dries the floor of the sea so the people can walk through it. And when Pharaoh's army follows,

God closes the sea over them. An impossible escape route is made possible. Just as he said he would, God delivers his people from their pursuing enemies. He delivers them from enslavement, from torture, from their very real fear of death.

I start here with the wonders in Egypt and Moses splitting the Red Sea because this is Joshua's testimony. Joshua watched all of this. He saw God's mighty power and his faithfulness. He experienced God's miraculous salvation. And this wasn't even all of it. On top of the wonders done in Egypt and the splitting of the sea, Joshua had eaten bread from heaven and drunk water out of rocks. He'd followed a real and actual pillar of cloud by day and a pillar of fire by night through the wilderness. Joshua had seen some pretty wild stuff. God had provided for him. Every. Single. Time. I write all that backstory to show you who God was to Joshua—strong, faithful, reliable, his deliverer and provider in times of need.

Joshua's Most-Played Track

As we catch up with Joshua, he is about to step into his new role as leader of the Israelites. God is commanding him to lead the people into the land of Canaan, the land God promised to give to his people hundreds of years before. Yet, in order to fulfill these promises, Joshua needs to take over the fortified city of Jericho. As Joshua and the people stare down their impossible situation, the words that ring out over them are the words of our verse. And they aren't spoken once; instead, like my AC/DC song on repeat, these words are spoken over and over again to Joshua and to the people as an anthem. I want you to hear them each in their context.

Right before Moses steps down as leader, he tells the people:

> "Be strong and courageous. Do not be afraid or terrified because of them, for the Lord your God goes with you; he will never leave you nor forsake you" (Deuteronomy 31:6).

As Moses hands his leadership over to Joshua, he tells him:

> "Be strong and courageous, for you must go with this
> people into the land that the Lord swore to their ances-
> tors to give them. . . . The Lord himself goes before you
> and will be with you; he will never leave you nor forsake
> you. Do not be afraid; do not be discouraged" (Deuter-
> onomy 31:7–8).

On Joshua's inauguration day, God tells him:

> "Be strong and courageous, for you will bring the Israel-
> ites into the land I promised them on oath, and I myself
> will be with you" (Deuteronomy 31:23).

Right before Joshua leads the people into the promised land,
God tells him:

> "As I was with Moses, so I will be with you; I will never
> leave you nor forsake you. Be strong and courageous,
> because you will lead these people to inherit the land
> I swore to their ancestors to give them. Be strong and
> very courageous. . . . Have I not commanded you? Be
> strong and courageous. Do not be afraid; do not be dis-
> couraged, for the Lord your God will be with you wher-
> ever you go" (Joshua 1:5–7, 9).

When Joshua tells the people the plan to go into the promised land, they respond by saying:

> "Only may the Lord your God be with you as he was
> with Moses. . . . Only be strong and courageous!" (Joshua
> 1:17–18).

Moses said it. God said it. The people said it. Again and again,
Joshua heard these words spoken over him and the people he was
charged to lead: be strong and courageous!

Of all the things that could have been said, why this specific command? God could have encouraged them with any words, so why these ones, and why on repeat? I think it's because Joshua was an ordinary person just like us. And people are wired to go to fear when the world pushes in, when our circumstances get complicated, when the unknown seems like a black abyss. Our heart pounds, our mind races, our spirit gets all tangled because we know our own limitations. We struggle with those negative thoughts on repeat, telling us our situation is impossible. So, we need a repetitious calling back of our mind, our spirit, our heart, and our body to be strong and courageous. We need to remind ourselves, *a lot*, to be strong and courageous. This is what we need, and this is what Joshua needed too. He needed God's truth on repeat, calling him to strength and courage. But look at what else is in there. Look at this list of promises.

God will never leave you or forsake you.
The LORD himself goes before you.
God will be with you wherever you go.
As God was with Moses, so he will be with you.

Joshua's courage and strength weren't dependent on him. They were dependent on the God who is reliable, who would always be with him, doing the very same kinds of things he did for Moses. God would never forsake him. God himself would lead the way. Joshua's courage and strength came from the Lord, and the same is true for us today. We aren't called to be strong and courageous in a vacuum. No. We can take courage because God is with us, and he will always be with us. Period.

What does this mean practically? My strength and bravery aren't dependent on my toughness, my power, or my ability to dig down deep and pull myself up by my own bootstraps. No, I am strong and courageous *because.* I am strong and courageous *because* the One who has always come through, has always been strong, has never been tired, has never feared, and has never, ever failed is with me. He is with me. And he promises he will never leave me. Joshua knew that. It was his song on repeat, and he believed it. But do we?

Here's What We Do

A few years back, my brother-in-law told me that our family has some of the strongest God-believing people he's ever known. But he was surprised at how often fear snuck into our language and the rhythm of our lives. Sure, we believed in God, we knew God, we loved God, but we oftentimes lacked trust in God when things got tough, even though we'd seen him show up so many times before! Yup. He was right. Humans are incredibly forgetful beings, of which I am most guilty. I forget all that God has done for me, all the times he has delivered me, sustained me, provided for me, and come through for me. I look at my situation, and I trade all that history in for fear. But if I look at what God's people did way back then, I find some really practical things I can do now to trade my fear in for courage.

> I forget all that God has done for me, all the times he has delivered me, sustained me, provided for me, and come through for me. I look at my situation, and I trade all that history in for fear.

Remember God's Faithfulness

The Israelites in the Bible are really just like me, guilty of exchanging their trust in a good, reliable, perfect God for fear. But God, in his kindness and knowledge of just how forgetful and weak they are, repeatedly reminds them of all he has done. He has them take part in special meals and sets up yearly ceremonies to help them recall dramatic events in their history. When God parts the Jordan River for the people to walk across into the promised land, he has them take stones from the center of the river and set them up as a memorial of his miraculous intervention. In these and in so many other ways, God establishes patterns of remembrance to remind them of his faithfulness. For example, just after God delivers the people out of Egypt, he tells them to have a yearly ceremonial meal:

> On that day tell your son, "I do this because of what the LORD did for me when I came out of Egypt." This observance will be for you like a sign on your hand and a reminder on your forehead that this law of the LORD is to be on your lips. For the LORD brought you out of Egypt with his mighty hand.
>
> Exodus 13:8–9

Just like God did for his people, we too can set up practices in our own lives like a sign on our hand, so every time we see it, we're reminded of God's faithful and "mighty hand."

Set Up Stones of Remembrance

At the height of the pandemic, we were all pretty dang afraid. In my greatest moments of fear, the *most* helpful thing I did (other than reading my Bible) was coach myself to remember all God had done for me. I got out a piece of paper and a pencil, and I listed out every one of my miracles. I wrote down every time God had come through when I needed him most, every time the impossible thing had happened, every time he provided me with more than I could imagine, every time I begged him to make a way, and he did. Even the good things I didn't know were miracles at the time but turned out for my good—I listed those too. They were one-word, one-line proofs of who God has been in my life. My boys. Pole vault. Dwell.

And then, I made another list on another piece of paper. I wrote out every single thing that was causing me to fear—just one word for each thing. COVID. Injustice. Death. I taped them to my kitchen wall. Every time I was afraid, I looked to my lists so I could *see* and remember. I needed physical cues of God's past faithfulness in order to coach my head and heart toward strength and courage in my current fears. My list of miracles hung on the wall for a year. And now it is a treasured piece of paper I keep in my bedside table. When fear comes knocking on my door, I don't hesitate to hang up my miracles and remind my heart of who is with me.

Trust God's Promises

Whenever my husband, Matt, and I are getting ready to go out on a date night, there's one thing I say over and over to one of my little sons. When I start putting on my makeup and can see him looking a little nervous, I remind him, "Mommy always comes back, buddy. I love you." As I put on my coat and he grabs my leg, I lean down and kiss him, squeeze him, and remind him, "Mommy always comes back." As we step over the threshold of the front door and he comes for one more hug, for one more "hold me," I say, "Mommy always what, Jordan?" And his sweet little strong voice says back to me, "Mommy always comes back." God does a similar thing for us, patiently reminding us that he is good and he is with us. *"I will never leave you. I will never forsake you. Even though you don't see me, I will be with you wherever you go."*

God's promises to us are even better than they were to Joshua. He told Joshua in our memory verse, "The Lord your God will be with you wherever you go" (Joshua 1:9), but Jesus expanded on this for his followers in the New Testament. Jesus promises not only to be *with* his followers but that the Holy Spirit would live *in* us. Here's what he says:

> And I will ask the Father, and he will give you another advocate to help you and be with you forever—the Spirit

of truth. . . . He lives with you and will be in you. . . . The Holy Spirit, whom the Father will send in my name, will teach you all things and will remind you of everything I have said to you. . . . Do not let your hearts be troubled and do not be afraid.

John 14:16–17, 26–27

Did you catch what Jesus says in that last verse? *"Do not let your hearts be troubled and do not be afraid."* Why? Because the Holy Spirit will be with you and in you. So, when I'm afraid (like my little buddy), when I want someone to be with *me* and never leave *me*, I am promised just that. Jesus tells us that the Holy Spirit is with us forever. He lives with us and in us, reminding us of everything that's true. Like a loving parent, God is gently whispering, "I am with you. I won't leave you. I won't forsake you. I will be with you wherever you go." Will we trust these promises? Our hearts can be strong and courageous because the Holy Spirit dwells in us, comforting and guiding us and never leaving us.

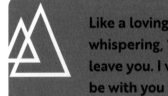

> Like a loving parent, God is gently whispering, "I am with you. I won't leave you. I won't forsake you. I will be with you wherever you go."

Treasure and Follow the Word

Smack-dab in the middle of our passage where God is calling the hearts of Joshua and his people up to strength and courage is a call to be in God's Word, day and night.

Be strong and very courageous. Be careful to obey all the law my servant Moses gave you; do not turn from it to the right or to the left, that you may be successful wherever you go. Keep this Book of the Law always on your lips; meditate on it day and night, so that you may be careful to do everything written in it. Then you will be prosperous and successful. Have I not commanded you? Be strong and courageous. Do not be afraid; do not be discouraged, for the LORD your God will be with you wherever you go.

Joshua 1:7–9

Do you see what I'm talking about? God says, "Be strong and very courageous. Obey and know the law. Be strong and courageous." There is something big for us in this! Be in God's Word. Isn't this again just exactly what we are encouraging you to do in this book?! When we are under stress, when we are afraid, when we start to panic, we should be going to God's true words to help us overcome our negative thought spirals.

But oftentimes we don't.

Instead, we follow the promises made by something else. In the midst of my fear and panic in the pandemic, I did a *lot* of treasuring the Word (especially Psalm 91), but I also did a lot of trusting in other things. Sometimes when I was afraid, I went to my news app, scanning the headlines for something that would save us all. I was tempted to eat the news all day, searching for truth and promises of deliverance. Eventually, when that did not satisfy my panic, I would recognize my wandering and I'd go back to Psalm 91. I reminded myself that instead of the government, "his faithfulness will be your shield and rampart" (Psalm 91:4).

In our Joshua passage, God says to know and obey his Word.

God tells the Israelites that in order to inherit the land, in order for them to be victorious, they would need to follow his Word, not turning away from it. We can't always know what success is going to look like for us in terms of the outcome of our circumstances. Sometimes our situations don't change. I didn't know if COVID was going to be the end of me (sometimes it felt like it was). But in my moments of fear, my strength and courage came from telling myself the truth of God's Word and believing it despite my

145

circumstances. In this passage, God tells Joshua (and us) not to depart from God's Word, because it is the place we can go to find courage in the face of our fear.

The Better Joshua

Joshua ran the race, he followed God, he remembered God's faithfulness, and he trusted in his promises, and God was faithful to lead him and the Israelites into the promised land. At the end of his road, when he was old and nearing death, Joshua looked back on his life, and what did he say to the people? He reminded them that all the good things they had seen in their lives were things God did. He told them to trust God's promises for their future. He told them to follow God's Word, to hold tight to God. And he told them, again, to be very strong.

Remember who God is.

Remember what God has done.

Trust God.

Follow God's Word.

Be strong and courageous.

Joshua gives us a fantastic example of how we can be victorious when we're facing real and scary situations. His life is a picture of God saving his people. In fact, his name even means *God is salvation.* In my study Bible, I read this and was blown away by the beauty and creativity of how God is always making a way for his people. "When this same name [Joshua] (the Greek form of which is Jesus . . .) was given to [Jesus], it identified him as the servant of God who would complete what God did for Israel in a preliminary way through the first Joshua, namely, overcome all powers of evil in the world and bring God's people into their eternal 'rest.'"[1] Joshua was the instrument God used to save his people from slavery and deliver them into the promised land. But Joshua was just a signpost, pointing to the better Joshua, Jesus, who saves us from our sin and leads us into eternal life with him.

Our current scary realities are real. Our fears are not without substance. But they don't have to take us captive. When we follow Jesus, we have ultimate victory over all that separates us from God, we receive salvation for our souls, and we will spend all eternity with him. For now, he tells us what I tell my own dear son: "I'll be back soon. I love you."

Apply the TRUTH

You can be strong and courageous, practically speaking.

Did you catch the list of things Joshua reminded his people of just before he left them? These are the things they needed to remember as they entered the scary new time when he'd be gone. So, I've got a super practical application for us. We are going to follow his list! Just like I had a list, you need a list—a reminder of truth to fight your fears. You can put it up on your fridge if you need it now or tuck it away for safekeeping when you need it later.

Remember Who God Is

Grab a pen and paper and write down every awesome thing you can think of about who God is. Write down some of the things you've learned in this chapter or some of your favorite verses about who he is and what he has done for you in Christ Jesus.

Remember What God Has Done

List out your miracles. List any ways that God has been specifically good or gracious to you. Write down the storms he's carried you through. Anything that builds your faith as you remember

God, write it down. Keep it simple: one word or sentence is plenty. Post that list where you can see it.

Trust God

God is trustworthy. The right, safe place for your confidence. Write out all the ways you know that God is worthy of your trust. Start right here with the promises he made to Joshua.

God will never leave me.

God will never forsake me.

God is with me wherever I go.

Follow God's Word

Now spend some time finding other promises for your life. Check out Psalm 91 if you don't know where to start. It is *fire*! It's written by Moses, who saw God do some pretty amazing things! List out every declaration Moses makes in his song. Keep going back to this psalm or find other promises in Scripture to list out.

Be Strong and Courageous

Make this verse your own personal anthem on repeat! Memorize it. Sing it. Write it on your mirror. Call your heart up into a brave trust in the God who is with you and even lives in you. Let it be your soundtrack of strength and courage: "Have I not commanded you? Be strong and courageous. Do not be afraid; do not be discouraged, for the LORD your God will be with you wherever you go" (Joshua 1:9).

HAVE I NOT
COMMANDED YOU?
BE STRONG AND COURAGEOUS.
DO NOT BE AFRAID;
DO NOT BE DISCOURAGED,
FOR THE LORD YOUR GOD
WILL BE WITH YOU
WHEREVER YOU GO.
JOSHUA 1:9

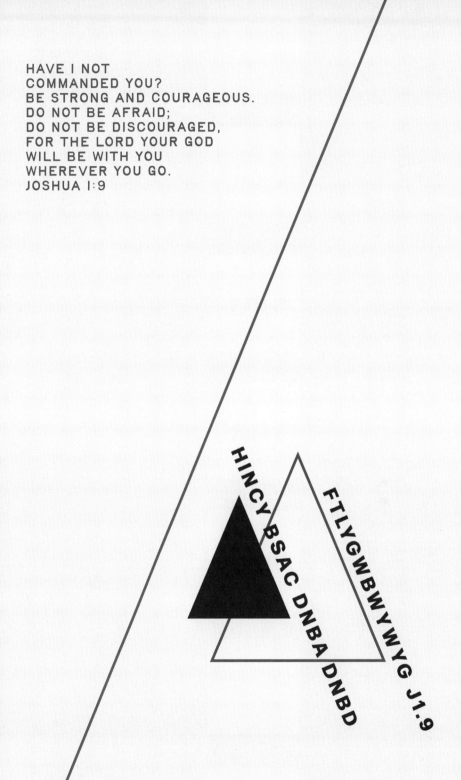

HINCY BSAC DNBA DNBD

FTLYGWBWYWYG J1.9

smy

wLt

myp

P25.4

SHOW ME YOUR WAYS, LORD. TEACH ME YOUR PATHS.
PSALM 25:4

9

TRUTH When You Need DIRECTION

NATALIE

Show me your ways, LORD, teach me your paths.
—Psalm 25:4

I Needed Direction

It all started with a bellyache.

On Monday, my daughter Esti called me from her high school. She and her brother had just parked when she threw up in the parking lot. She said her stomach hurt, "But not that bad." She thought maybe she ate something funny. She said she was fine to go to class. *Hmmm . . . Should I just go and get her?* About an hour later she texted that her belly "really hurts" and she wanted to come home. Of course, I went and picked her up. But once we were home, she seemed fine. I asked if her belly still hurt. "Not really anymore. Maybe it's just cramps. . . ." *Okay. Whatever.* I felt a little duped. *Should I have taken her out of school? Still, maybe she's sick or something. And if it IS just cramps, I mean, I get it.* But I started to get that nagging mom feeling in my gut, like something was wrong but I wasn't sure what. *Maybe it's nothing.*

On Tuesday morning, her belly hurt again, and she asked to stay home. *Sure.* By eleven o'clock though, she felt better and wanted

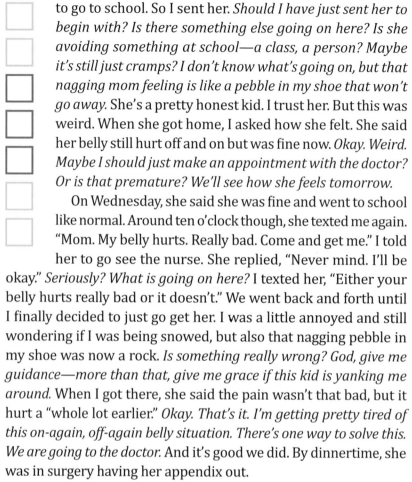

to go to school. So I sent her. *Should I have just sent her to begin with? Is there something else going on here? Is she avoiding something at school—a class, a person? Maybe it's still just cramps? I don't know what's going on, but that nagging mom feeling is like a pebble in my shoe that won't go away.* She's a pretty honest kid. I trust her. But this was weird. When she got home, I asked how she felt. She said her belly still hurt off and on but was fine now. *Okay. Weird. Maybe I should just make an appointment with the doctor? Or is that premature? We'll see how she feels tomorrow.*

On Wednesday, she said she was fine and went to school like normal. Around ten o'clock though, she texted me again. "Mom. My belly hurts. Really bad. Come and get me." I told her to go see the nurse. She replied, "Never mind. I'll be okay." *Seriously? What is going on here?* I texted her, "Either your belly hurts really bad or it doesn't." We went back and forth until I finally decided to just go get her. I was a little annoyed and still wondering if I was being snowed, but also that nagging pebble in my shoe was now a rock. *Is something really wrong? God, give me guidance—more than that, give me grace if this kid is yanking me around.* When I got there, she said the pain wasn't that bad, but it hurt a "whole lot earlier." *Okay. That's it. I'm getting pretty tired of this on-again, off-again belly situation. There's one way to solve this. We are going to the doctor.* And it's good we did. By dinnertime, she was in surgery having her appendix out.

Writing all of that just made me cry.

I cried in relief that my sweet girl Esti is doing just fine. I cried in gratitude to God for his guidance and care. I cried because that was actually a lot, and I didn't realize it until now. I cried because I needed to release all the tension and stress of making hard decisions.

We Need Direction

This isn't just me in this one rare instance needing direction. It's all of us. We all make decisions every single day. And we need direction—not just in those big one-time things but in all the little daily choices we make. Let me give you just a tiny peek behind the curtain at the vast number of decisions many of us face every day.

Do I keep renting or buy a place?

Is this in my best interest?

Should I commit or should I wait?

Do I take the first step, or will that seem desperate?

Is this the right school for me, for my kid?

Should I fix this car or get a new one?

If I say yes to this, what will I be saying no to?

Do I look for a new job? Do I take it?

Do I move? Should I stay?

Where should I invest my money?

What do I want to be when I grow up?

What do I *really* want to be now that I am a "grown-up"?

Is this good for me? Is it right? Right now?

These are just some of the questions rattling around in our heads on any given day. They can be as insignificant as "Where do we go for dinner?" and as impactful as "Where do we go now?" All of these choices can lead to decision overwhelm, fatigue, and even paralysis. We can't know every possible outcome. So, how do we know what to do?

Sometimes we just throw our hands in the air and ask, "God, what do I do?!"

And this is *it*! This is actually the place we need to get to—the end of ourselves. It's when we acknowledge we can't know the right decision that we finally get to the place where we ask God to help us. But shouldn't we always be asking? Doesn't it make sense that in our limited human abilities we *should* go to the limitless God of all things and ask for help? And here's the mind-boggling truth—God *wants* us to go to him. He knows our limits. He knows we simply don't have the insight, wisdom, or ability to always do what's best, no matter how much we desire to do so or how hard we try. So, God in his loving mercy says, "Ask me for help."

When we are uncertain about the future, he wants to give us insight.

When we feel overwhelmed, he wants to help us find peace.

When our negative thoughts paralyze us, God wants to help us take the next right step.

When we are exhausted from spinning our gears, he gives us real rest.

In Psalm 25, God's man David models the right way for humans to make decisions, and it all starts with throwing up our hands and saying, "Show me *your* ways, LORD, teach me *your* paths" (v. 4, emphasis added). Let's read the whole psalm so we can take a closer look at how to go to God for direction in our lives.

Psalm 25
Of David.

1 In you, LORD my God,
I put my trust.

2 I trust in you;
do not let me be put to shame,
nor let my enemies triumph over me.
3 No one who hopes in you
will ever be put to shame,
but shame will come on those
who are treacherous without cause.

4 Show me your ways, LORD,
teach me your paths.
5 Guide me in your truth and teach me,
for you are God my Savior,
and my hope is in you all day long.

---

6 Remember, Lord, your great mercy and love,
for they are from of old.
7 Do not remember the sins of my youth
and my rebellious ways;
according to your love remember me,
for you, Lord, are good.

8 Good and upright is the Lord;
therefore he instructs sinners in his ways.
9 He guides the humble in what is right
and teaches them his way.
10 All the ways of the Lord are loving and faithful
toward those who keep the demands of his covenant.
11 For the sake of your name, Lord,
forgive my iniquity, though it is great.

12 Who, then, are those who fear the Lord?
He will instruct them in the ways they should choose.
13 They will spend their days in prosperity,
and their descendants will inherit the land.
14 The Lord confides in those who fear him;
he makes his covenant known to them.
15 My eyes are ever on the Lord,
for only he will release my feet from the snare.

16 Turn to me and be gracious to me,
for I am lonely and afflicted.
17 Relieve the troubles of my heart
and free me from my anguish.
18 Look on my affliction and my distress
and take away all my sins.
19 See how numerous are my enemies
and how fiercely they hate me!

20 Guard my life and rescue me;
do not let me be put to shame,
for I take refuge in you.
21 May integrity and uprightness protect me,
because my hope, Lord, is in you.

22 Deliver Israel, O God,
from all their troubles!

Let's Dive In

I love David's heart in this psalm. He lays it all out before the Lord. He goes to God with his honest struggle, telling him that he needs help. In fact, he recognizes that *only* God can help. And because of who God is, he is trusting that God will hear him and rescue him. Really, that's it. That's all this psalm is about. And yet, there's just so much goodness here for us to discover. And I want you to see exactly what I'm talking about, so I'm going to ask you to go back through Psalm 25 and mark every time David talks about each of these three things:

1. Underline every time he says something about who God is.
2. Put a box around all the ways David is trusting or looking to God.
3. Circle all the requests he makes of God.

Did you see that? Psalm 25 is really about these three interrelated things: because David knows God, he trusts God, and because he trusts God, David asks God for help. Let's look at them each in turn.

Know God

■ God Is Unchangingly God

In this psalm we see that David is in the thick of it; he has no idea what to do. He needs someone bigger, smarter, and stronger than himself. David needs God to show up and show him his ways! He knows that God is the only one who can help him, his only hope. Though he feels lonely and afflicted (v. 16), he knows that God hasn't abandoned him and will help him. Why? Because though David's situation is changeful and uncertain, God is unchangingly himself. So David reminds himself of all the ways that God is God. Did you see it there in the psalm? Is your Psalm 25 page like mine? Full of underlined truths proclaiming who God is? If we boil down what David says, we see two overarching themes about God: he is good, and he helps his people.

■ God Is Good

Well, of course he is! And this is the place where we'd be tempted to give a quick nod and move on. But let's linger here instead. David does. Even though David's life is full of uncertainties and difficulties, David tells God that he is good. But he isn't telling God anything God doesn't already know about himself. Rather, David tells God that he is "good and upright" (v. 8) because he is relying on that goodness in spite of his situation. David says that God is "loving and faithful toward those who keep the demands of his covenant" (v. 10) because he needs God to be loving and faithful to him. He asks God to "remember . . . your great mercy and love" (v. 6) because he needs that mercy and love right now. Can you relate? I can. When things get bad and I am uncertain about what to do, I'm comforted with the truth that God is good and his goodness is reliable and unchanging, unlike my uncertain and changeful circumstances.

■ God Helps His People

God's willingness to aid his people isn't just a separate aspect of his character. Rather, it is intertwined with his goodness. In fact, it's precisely because he is good that he helps his people. Notice what David says: "Good and upright is the LORD; *therefore* he instructs sinners in his ways" (v. 8, emphasis added). *Because* God is good and upright, he helps sinners. This is why David asks God for help, because that's just who God is.

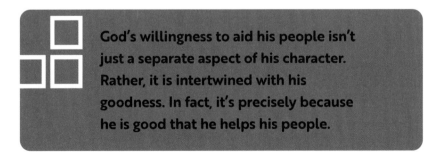

> God's willingness to aid his people isn't just a separate aspect of his character. Rather, it is intertwined with his goodness. In fact, it's precisely because he is good that he helps his people.

157

There's a pattern here I want you to see.

Again and again, David asks for a specific kind of help, and in the same breath he tells God he is helpful in that specific way. For example, in verses 2 and 3, David says, "Do not let me be put to shame. . . . No one who hopes in you will ever be put to shame." He asks God for the very thing he tells God he is specifically good at doing. And because David's main ask is for guidance, he really enumerates all the ways that God lovingly leads his people. David says that God instructs sinners in his ways, guides and teaches the humble in what is right, instructs his followers in the ways they should choose, makes his covenant known to them, and confides in those who fear him. In all of this David is telling God, "You are a God who does all of these things for those who follow you! And I follow you, Lord. So, help me." David can be confident that God will help him because God always helps his people. It's just who he is. Like David, we too can rely on God to be unchangingly himself. Because God is good and helps his people, we can and should trust him.

Trust God

If God is eternally good and upright, always loving and faithful, never-ending in his mercy, willing and able to help, then our only logical human response is to trust him. And this is precisely what David does. I love how David sprinkles this entire psalm with *trust*. Did you note all these instances on your copy of the psalm? Let me remind you of them here:

- "In you, LORD my God, I put my trust" (v. 1).
- "I trust in you" (v. 2).
- "You are God my Savior, and my hope is in you all day long" (v. 5).
- "My eyes are ever on the LORD, for only he will release my feet from the snare" (v. 15).

- "I take refuge in you" (v. 20).
- "My hope, LORD, is in you" (v. 21).

They're such good words to hide in our hearts or at least put in our back pocket for later, aren't they? I'd encourage you to memorize at least one of these other verses along with our verse for this chapter. They are short, simple phrases we can say to tell our God "I trust in you." Amen?

David's faith is expressed in his focus.

Throughout David's conversation with God, he likens his life to being on a journey—"Show me your *ways*, LORD, teach me your *paths*" (v. 4, emphasis added). He uses the word *way* five other times in this short psalm. And though he is on a path trying to decipher his next step, it's not the path that he's focused on, it's his guide. He isn't trusting in the infallibility of his own steps but in the one who's leading him. Notice what he says in verse 15: "My eyes are ever on the LORD, for only he will release my feet from the snare." We know from the context that right now David is completely tripped up. But instead of fixating on the problem, he fixes his eyes on the Lord. David confesses that only God can and *will* release his feet from the snare.

It reminds me of Peter walking on water.

Jesus calls him out of the boat to walk with him on water. Yes, *water*! But Peter steps out, and as long as he keeps his focus on Jesus, Peter's actually doing the impossible, walking on water! But once he starts to notice that wind picking up, his heart loses courage and he starts to sink. Our lesson here is this: instead of focusing on our problems, instead of fixating on our negative thoughts about how everything could all fall apart, we should keep our eyes "ever on the LORD" (v. 15), knowing only he can lead us on the otherwise impossible path. Only he is able to release our feet from the things that trip us up. So why keep focusing on all those negative thoughts? Instead, let's look to our God, who is trustworthy and will deliver us.

Ask God

Because God is good and helps his people, *and* because David trusts God, he takes action—he asks for help. Loads of help. Did you circle all the ways David asks God for help? It was a lot, right? He says, "God, please don't do this, instead do that, don't remember this, do remember that, show me, teach me, guide me, forgive me, free me, see me, rescue me, protect me," and on and on. To sum it all up, David has thrown up his hands and thrown in his lot with God, the only one who can help him. I love how David acts on his trust in God's character by asking him for help. David is a model of how our knowledge should support our faith, which should lead to action. But before we move on, I want you to see just exactly how he asks God for help and how God responds.

■ Ask in Humility

Remember who David said God helps? "Good and upright is the LORD; therefore he instructs *sinners* in his ways. He guides the *humble* in what is right and teaches them his way" (vv. 8–9, emphasis added). God's not instructing and guiding those smug self-righteous people who have it all buttoned up. They'd never ask God for the help that they don't think they need anyway. No, God helps humble sinners—the people who know they need help, the ones who are fully aware that they can't do it on their own. Those are the people who rely on God. Similarly, in the New Testament, Jesus tells the self-righteous religious leaders of his day, "It is not the healthy who need a doctor, but the sick. . . . For I have not come to call the righteous, but sinners" (Matthew 9:12–13). It's only when we recognize our sin and need that we come to God for help. So, we see David confess his sins three times, saying, "Do not remember the sins of my youth and my rebellious ways," "forgive my iniquity," and "take away all my sins" (vv. 7, 11, 18). David humbly and sincerely confesses his waywardness, knowing God forgives sinners and puts their feet back on the right path. This is the best news, isn't it?! God's only condition for helping us isn't our flawless record of good choices but our humble acknowledgment of our bad choices. Whew. That's some good news right there!

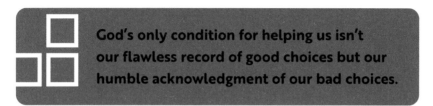

God's only condition for helping us isn't our flawless record of good choices but our humble acknowledgment of our bad choices.

■ Ask for Help with Others

David may have penned this psalm on his own when he felt lonely and troubled (v. 16), but this prayer song isn't meant for a soloist to sing but a full choir. Like we learned in chapter 7, the Psalms are the songbook of the church, sung by all believers for all time. So, for thousands of years God's people have together cried out for his direction and help by way of this song. At the end, David makes this prayer for all of God's people, saying, "Deliver Israel, O God, from all their troubles!" (v. 22). There is a corporate nature of asking God for help. Although David may have felt all alone, he simply was not. And though we may feel all alone and uncertain in our decisions, we are not alone either. God has given us other believers to come alongside us and seek his direction together. God has given us pastors and elders to shepherd us. He has given us beloved friends and mentors to walk with us. He has gifted some to be counselors to wisely advise us along the way. God is not calling us to a lonely path but to one that we can travel together as he lights the way.

■ God Will Respond

Okay, so this is it! This is the thing you've been waiting for. How does God respond? When you come to the one true God of everything, trusting him to forgive your mess and asking him for direction, what does he give you? Guidance and goodness! Here's what our psalm says: "Who, then, are those who fear the LORD? He will instruct them in the ways they should choose. They will spend their days in prosperity, and their descendants will inherit the land" (vv. 12–13). David says God gives his followers instruction, prosperity, and inheritance. These are all the fulfillments of the promises God made to his Old Testament followers. They were promised a physical land and physical abundance.

But what about us? Is God going to give us a property deed? As New Testament believers, actual physical land isn't a part of it. We instead are given a spiritual inheritance, we look forward to a restored new heavens and earth, and right now we have every spiritual blessing in Christ (read Ephesians 1:3–14 for more on this). Still, there is something else here in the psalm for us to discover, a blessing beyond the physical land that God gives his Old Testament followers, a blessing that is even fuller for us New Testament believers. God himself whispers mysteries in our ears. Verse 14 (emphasis added) says, "The LORD *confides* in those who fear him; he makes his covenant known to them." It is not enough that God is good and upright, abounding in mercy toward sinners, forgiving and guiding their paths. It's not enough either that God lavishes abundant blessings on those who follow him. On top of all this, God *confides* in his people.

Did you get that?!

God, *the* God of all the universe, who is all powerful, all knowing, who is glorious and enthroned in heaven on the endless praises of perfect heavenly beings, *this* God draws us near, close enough to whisper his mysteries in our ears. He *confides* in us, in David, in you, in me. He not only tells us the next step we should take, he tells us *why*! He tells us his secrets—he's opened up for us the glories of his mysterious plan to redeem a broken, willful people, to call us his own, to give us a seat at his table and to feast forever with him. He has not just put our feet on the

path that leads to him, he confides in us and reveals to us his reasoning. And it is baffling! He loves us. He wants us. He is calling us to be with him. And he hasn't left us alone on the journey home. He is ever with us, even in us, guiding our every step. This is our God—*the* God, who is God, who is worthy of our trust and devotion, who hears and answers his beloved children so that we can be with him. Know this God in your mind, trust him in your heart, and follow him with your feet. And whenever you come to a fork in the road, ask God for guidance, just like David did. "Show me your ways, LORD, teach me your paths" (Psalm 25:4).

Apply the TRUTH

- Tell about a time when you threw up your hands and said, "Show me your ways, LORD, teach me your paths!" What was the result?
- Where do you need guidance right now?
- How have you gone your own way? Ask God to forgive you and give you courage and strength to follow his path.
- List out the requests you have and the corresponding traits of God that speak to your specific needs (for example: Lord, please show me your paths—you always guide your followers in the way they should go).
- What negative thoughts do you have regarding your ability to make decisions? (*I am going to make the wrong choice* or *I never know what to do.*) Write out how God's truth combats these lies.
- How does knowing that God *wants* to guide you give you confidence in your decision-making?
- Write out a prayer telling God who he is and why you trust him, and then ask him to help you follow him in your choices.

- Find time in the next day or two to listen to this chapter's podcast episode about decision-making.

Practical Decision-Making Guide

Like we discussed at the very beginning of this chapter, making decisions is the air we breathe, minute by minute, day by day. So, I want to give you a practical decision-making guide right here—a quick reference you can easily come back to when you're trying to make a call on what to do.

1. **Remember who God is.** This is the foundation for every decision. Remember those aspects of God's character that specifically speak to your situation. Allow his control and knowledge and power over all things to give you peace.
2. **Ask God for guidance.** We all go our own ways, all the time. When you find yourself on your own path, just apologize and ask God for help getting back on his path.
3. **Remember God's Word.** God is pretty clear about what his path looks like. So much of what we labor to decide is already decided in God's Word. If his Word says *yes*, it is a *yes*. If his Word says *no*, it is a *no*.
4. **Ask other believers.** When both paths you could choose are a *yes*, it's time to phone a friend. Ask your pastor, your mentor, your close friend, or your counselor for guidance and prayer.
5. **Trust the answer.** Like we discovered, God's best answer is always himself. Yes, he has a good specific path for your life, and it is good to seek him and follow his path. But the real joy of the journey is traveling with him and knowing that he isn't just your guide but your destination.

smy

wLt

myp

P25.4

SHOW ME YOUR WAYS, LORD, TEACH ME YOUR PATHS.
PSALM 25:4

itswtShuiowwdnkwwotpfbtShifutwg R8.26

IN THE
SAME WAY,
THE SPIRIT
HELPS US
IN OUR
WEAKNESS.
WE DO NOT
KNOW WHAT
WE OUGHT TO
PRAY FOR,
BUT THE
SPIRIT
HIMSELF
INTERCEDES
FOR US
THROUGH
WORDLESS
GROANS.
ROMANS 8:26

10

TRUTH When You CAN'T PRAY

VERA

In the same way, the Spirit helps us in our weakness. We do not know what we ought to pray for, but the Spirit himself intercedes for us through wordless groans.

—Romans 8:26

When There Are No Words

My cursor is blinking at me as I try to begin this chapter. I got up early, before the kids, made the coffee, and sat down to write. But then I busied myself with other work. It's because I struggle to know what to say. Ironically, this chapter is to help you when you don't have anything to say to God. It's truth for when you can't pray, when you don't know what to pray, when you are past words. And so, naturally, what I am about to write about are some of my most difficult times, moments when I've been past words.

On February 15, 2021, I got a frantic call from one of my best friends, Lauren. Her husband, Brian, a state trooper, had been hit and was being airlifted to the hospital. There had been a snowstorm that day, and he was going to stop home during his shift to change out his soaked-through boots. He had told Lauren that there was a chance that, if things weren't too bad, he'd be able to clock out early. But on the way home, he'd stopped as backup on a crash site. While Brian helped shut down the lane so that vehicles would drive around the accident, his patrol vehicle was hit from behind by someone who failed to move over. We'd find out in the next few hours that he had sustained a traumatic brain injury.

I could tell you a thousand happy stories of Lauren and Brian. Their kind, funny, easy-to-be-around personalities are addictive. They are some of the truest people I know . . . like, down-to-earth, real, *real* humans. They make you feel special, like you are the only friend they have. They make you feel like a champion, supporting your any and every thing. They make you want to be near them, because to be near them is to be loved big. I could fill this whole book with laughter and love if I were to tell you of the two of them, and my cursor would continue to fly down the page, one story after the next.

In the moments following Lauren's call, I had not *one* word. I can remember kneeling on the floor in my room weeping, and my mind was all messed up. Everything felt vividly clear but totally blurred at the same time.

The next few days, weeks, months, years are all a blur. Brian is still in a minimally conscious state. I do not have words for the pain and suffering Lauren and Brian have endured. Occasionally, there are the brief thoughts that sit in my mind, like *Why? How? How long?* When those thoughts come, I march them straight to God and let him hold them. And then I find myself, again, without any words at all.

For me, these last few years have been some of my most word-less times praying to God. For some of you, suffering and loss have also left you speechless, unable to go before God in prayer. For others, maybe it's something else that is rendering you unable to pray.

Maybe you've never prayed before, so how do you even start?

Maybe it's been a long time since you prayed, and you hesitate to start out of guilt.

Maybe you feel you need to clean things up in your life before you can talk to this big, holy, perfect God.

Maybe you're afraid that some of those negative thoughts swirling around in your head will come out and shock God.

Or maybe you have a hard decision to make, and you're torn on what to even pray *for*.

Maybe you're mad at God.

Or maybe you're just too tired or worn-down to even go there.

Before we get into the verse for this chapter, I want to share some practical things I've learned for times when I can't pray. Normally, I save this type of thing for the end of a chapter, but I think it is better to start here.

How to Pray When You Don't Know What to Pray

Simply Call on God

The Bible tells us, "The LORD is near to all who call on him, to all who call on him in truth" (Psalm 145:18). God is near to anyone and everyone who calls on him in earnest. Here is what that might look like, practically. You don't have to be an expert. Just call on him. Maybe pray something like this:

God, you say you are near to anyone who might call on you. I am asking you to hear me now. I feel alone. I'm without words or understanding or wisdom for my situation—without clarity or insight into what I should do. I am me, with very little to offer. Here I am. Will you meet me here?

When you're done, it's okay to just be with him in your silence, waiting to see if more words come. Maybe they do, and maybe they don't. If you have feelings or thoughts that do come, simply tell them to him. He wants them all. He can handle them all. Even those negative thoughts, the ones that aren't good or right, even when you're mad at him. He can take them all. He can bear it all. God *wants* to be near you. He *will* be near to you, even in your silence. Sitting in silence with him is a great place to start.

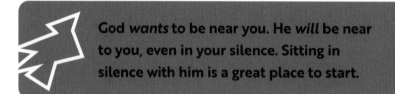

> God *wants* to be near you. He *will* be near to you, even in your silence. Sitting in silence with him is a great place to start.

Let Scripture Be Your Words When You Don't Have Any

The Bible is full of every type of person and every type of prayer, and we are meant to plagiarize its words. If you aren't used to picking up the Bible, the book of Psalms is a perfect place to go when you have nothing to say. There are prayers of praise, suffering, fear, frustration, anguish, confession . . . you name it, it's in there. Let the prayers in Scripture be your prayers. Let its words be your words.

Psalms for When You Don't Have Words

Psalm 16—God will never abandon me
Psalm 27—I will wait for God
Psalm 63—My soul thirsts for God
Psalm 91—God is my refuge
Psalm 139—God knows my heart

Brevity Is Okay

My husband was recently listening to a podcast called *Dad Tired*, and the host reminded his listeners that when Jesus prayed, it was often brief. We don't need a PhD in prayer, we just need to talk to Jesus. Be set free from any expectations you think he might have for length or smartness of words. In fact, Jesus once called out a bunch of religious people for praying a bunch of smart, wordy, lengthy prayers (Matthew 6:5–7). Again, he just wants you.

Ask Someone Else to Pray for You

Can I confess something to you right now? This book has been a challenging endeavor for me. I've never written anything like this before, and today I felt overwhelmed by the weight of it all. I just went downstairs to make myself a coffee, and as I stood in the kitchen waiting for it to be ready, all I wanted was for someone to pray for me! I could hear my babysitter playing with my son Jordan in the next room over, and I wanted to go ask her to pray for me. But, inside my head, there was this tiny whisper: "Do you *really* need that?" I almost didn't go. I almost marched back up to my office. But then I decided to ask her. And her prayer, on my behalf, was like a balm to my soul. I cried. I felt at peace. And here I am, back to writing. May I remind you that when we pray with other believers, Jesus is right there with us (Matthew 18:20). Ask someone to pray for you when you can't pray.

Pray Like Jesus Taught Us to Pray

For many of us, we learned this rote prayer as kids, and maybe it has lost its luster. But the prayer laid out to us by Jesus is a perfect way to just get going. Here is how you might pray the Lord's Prayer.

> ***Our father who art in heaven, hallowed be thy name***
> Praise God for who he is and how you've seen him work in your life, in the lives of others, and in his creation all around you.

Thy kingdom come, thy will be done, on earth as it is in heaven
Ask God to open your eyes to his will and the eternal things happening around you.
Give us this day our daily bread
Ask God to provide for your needs. Share with him a physical, emotional, or spiritual thing you need most today.
And forgive us our trespasses
Ask God to reveal where you've made something else greater than him.
As we forgive those who trespass against us
Ask God to help you to be gracious in your interactions with others, since he is so gracious to you.
And lead us not into temptation
Ask God to be near, leading you in every detail of your day. Share with him a specific thing you need his leading in today.
But deliver us from evil
Ask for protection from the enemy. Ask him to guard your mind and your spirit from any evil thing put against you.

In seasons of wordlessness, you can start with any of these little prompts to help you. Tear these pages right out of this book and keep them at the ready. Or just turn down the corner of this page. Either way, I want to encourage you to just start. (If you want an even more in-depth way to *personally* pray the Lord's Prayer, see this blog post.[1])

But What If I Still Can't Pray?

Following Brian's accident, more than seventy friends and family members of Brian and Lauren would gather over Zoom to pray each week. I remember waiting for that first scheduled prayer call and feeling nervous because I thought I had *nothing* to pray, nothing that I could add. I felt the pressure of wanting to say the right thing to encourage Lauren, to bring God's hope, to be a light in the darkness. But anything I could pray felt like it was going to be too much or not enough—any words that I could offer felt completely inadequate.

I lay on the rug in our play room, with the door locked so no children could come in, and decided to do the one thing I knew how to do. I opened up my Bible. As a side note, if ever you are in a moment of crisis, or maybe you feel like your time in God's Word has become a duty instead of a delight, don't be afraid to go back to the passages of Scripture that really speak to you. I do this often. And for me, one of those passages is Romans chapter 8. I opened up the Bible and began to read. "In the same way, the Spirit helps us in our weakness. We do not know what we ought to pray for, but the Spirit himself intercedes for us through wordless groans" (Romans 8:26).

Right there, in my moment of speechlessness, in my moment of need, I was reminded that my inadequacy was all I needed. My weakness and speechlessness were even biblical, "*We do not know what we ought to pray for . . .*" and God had not left me without recourse. I was not alone before God—he'd given me his Holy Spirit. When I had not one word, the Holy Spirit would pray *for me.*

He would intervene on my behalf.

And so, this is the prayer I prayed alongside seventy other speechless people.

Holy Spirit, be with us. We are empty, scared, without words, eager for you to pray for us. You help us when we are weak. You go to the Father for us when we have not one word. Please, pray now for us, for Brian, for Lauren. Express for us every need we have, every pain we feel, every ache of our soul. When we have nothing but tears and cries from the pit of our soul, Holy Spirit, you will carry it all to the Father for us.

And the words kept coming. Out of my emptiness and weakness came prayer. Out of my trust and belief that the Holy Spirit was at work came hope and encouragement.

The Holy Spirit Helps Us

The Holy Spirit is the powerful person of God who lives in any and every person who believes and accepts Jesus. Romans chapter 8, where we find our verse, is all about him. The book of Romans is a letter written by Paul to the new believers in Rome, and in chapter 8, we get this powerful pump-up section where we learn all about what our life should look like in the power of the Holy Spirit. Here are just a few things that the Holy Spirit does in the believer.

He comforts us.

He is our helper.

He convicts us.

He guides us into all the truth.

He speaks to us.

He empowers us to share about Jesus.

He helps us have a deep knowledge of Jesus's love for us.

He helps illuminate Scripture when we read it.

He empowers us to overcome our sin.

He helps us have the character of Christ.

He gives gifts that we might be able to serve others and point them to Jesus.

And specifically, Romans 8, the chapter we are looking at, teaches us these things about the Spirit.

The power of the Holy Spirit gives us life (v. 2).

He helps us set our mind on true and good things (v. 5).

He brings us life and peace (v. 6).

He helps us to have power over sin (vv. 9, 13).

He guarantees our resurrection (v. 11).

He leads us (v. 14).

He testifies that we are children of God (vv. 14, 15, 16).

He helps us in our weakness (v. 26).

He intercedes for us (v. 26).

He goes to God for us in accordance with God's will (v. 27).

I grew up in a Christian tradition that didn't talk much about the Holy Spirit, and so for much of my early adult life, I was unaware of what strength and power I had *living right inside me*. Maybe that has been your experience too. So let me say this to you—the Holy Spirit, who is God, dwells in you, filling you, strengthening you, giving you power. When I close my eyes and imagine the Holy Spirit in me, I envision my inner being going from black-and-white to technicolor. He is in us, and he gives us every amazing thing! And when we have not one word to utter, he is going to God for us, praying for us. He fully knows us, and he fully knows the Father. He knows just what to say to communicate everything to him. Peace and rest are ours when we know all our needs and pain and loss and desires are brought before God by our comforter, the Holy Spirit.

When I close my eyes and imagine the Holy Spirit in me, I envision my inner being going from black-and-white to technicolor.

In Our Suffering

In the same way, the Spirit helps us in our weakness. We do not know what we ought to pray for, but the Spirit himself intercedes for us through wordless groans. And he who searches our hearts knows the mind of the Spirit, because the Spirit intercedes for God's people in accordance with the will of God. And we know that in all things God works for the good of those who love him, who have been called according to his purpose.

Romans 8:26–28

When we pray, or someone prays for us, the Holy Spirit intercedes for us and the burden of our situation is lifted, if only for a moment. But as our humanness takes back over and our eyes fix back on the problem, whether in the very next moment or the next day, we are left again in the overwhelm of whatever sorrow or unanswerable predicament we find ourselves in. And we are right to feel a deep ache, because our spirits know that this world isn't our home. We long for perfect bodies and perfect minds and no more tears or sorrow or suffering. We groan because we are in the in-between, just waiting for things to be made right. In fact, the actual physical world groans right along with us. Creation is aching to be made right. Every flower, tree, mountain, star, sea . . .

every cloud, every grain of sand, every last thing that we see groans and waits for us to be brought into perfection when everything will be made right! We are all holding our breath, waiting, and aching. It is no surprise, then, that the Spirit *groans too*, on our behalf. This suffering—it is not unseen, and your feelings are right. Our home isn't here.

But in that moment, when we feel all that is true about our temporary home here on earth, we must gather our tiny mustard-seed faith and try to believe and hope in this promise: God is working it all out for our good.

I have seen people make the mistake of telling someone who is *really in it* that "God is working it out for your good," casually flinging this phrase as a fix for their suffering. Though what they say is true, if it is said without the context of Jesus and his suffering, these words are salt on a wound, lacking the proper empathy. And so I say this to you now: Jesus knows your suffering. He knows your pain. He suffered a miserable, lonely death for me and you. He followed God's will and purposeful plan so that you and I might be made right with God. He does not despise or misunderstand you or your situation. God, in his love and mercy, didn't spare Jesus. He gave him over to death in order to work life and salvation and good in us (Romans 8:32).

And because we have Jesus and because he suffered for us, we can have hope in the promise that God is also working everything out for our good.

As We Wait

What, then, shall we say in response to these things? If God is for us, who can be against us? He who did not spare his own Son, but gave him up for us all—how will he not also, along with him, graciously give us all things? . . . Christ Jesus who died— more than that, who was raised to life—is at the right hand of God and is also interceding for us. Who shall separate us from the love of Christ? Shall trouble or hardship or persecution or famine or nakedness or danger or sword? . . . No, in all these things we are more than conquerors through him who loved us. For I am convinced that neither death nor life, neither angels nor demons, neither the present nor the future, nor any powers, neither height nor depth, nor anything else in all creation, will be able to separate us from the love of God that is in Christ Jesus our Lord.

Romans 8:31–32, 34–35, 37–39

177

We are still waiting. Brian isn't healed yet. We ache and groan and hope and pray wordless prayers along with Lauren for his body and mind to be woven back together. I continually lean into the Holy Spirit and his power and the promise that he is right there with me, praying for my friends. And I am not without hope. Can I share one more precious, *precious* truth with you from this passage? It only increases my hope. The same Jesus who suffered for us and who knows our pain is *also interceding for us.* Jesus, who was intimately acquainted with grief, is speaking directly to the Father about ours. When we go to God, we can go with confidence knowing these things. God meets us there. The Holy Spirit is there with us, aching our aches before God. And Jesus is there interceding, advocating, and pleading alongside us.

When we don't know what to pray, we can be assured that God meets us, his Spirit prays for us, and his Son intercedes for us. We are never alone in our time of need.

And we are not without comfort, because we are promised great things in our moments of need, trial, and despair. Let our hearts never forget these truths:

Nothing can separate us from the love of Jesus.

Death can't separate us from God's love.

This life can't separate us from God's love.

Nothing in the spiritual realm can separate us from God's love.

Nothing that is or will come can separate us from God's love.

No power or depth, *nothing* in creation can separate us from his love.

We are more than conquerors.

This is my final prayer; if you can't pray, let me pray for you.

May God's love wash over you. May your heart know that he is with you, and he is for you. "May the God of hope fill you with all joy and peace as you trust in him, so that you may overflow with hope by the power of the Holy Spirit" (Romans 15:13).

—————— Apply the TRUTH ——————

- What are some of the reasons you struggle to pray (either now or typically)?
- How are you freed by knowing you don't have to find the perfect words to say?
- How is it comforting to know that Jesus (who was a man of suffering) and the Holy Spirit are both with you and interceding for you in your prayers?
- On a piece of paper, list out your most difficult or longtime prayers. Now find a Scripture verse or passage that speaks to each prayer. Rework the words into a prayer for that person or situation. Write them out and keep that paper in your Bible or in a handy place for whenever you want to pray for those situations.
- How has God met you and grown your faith in those most difficult prayers? Thank him for his work in you.
- How have you struggled in your faith because of waiting for or wanting things you know God could give but has not? Tell God about it—all your anger, disappointment, and hurt. Ask him to meet you in those raw feelings and show you a way forward.
- Ask God for the right person to come alongside you and pray for you and support you in your most difficult prayer needs.

Listen to the podcast episode to hear more from Vera and Natalie about times when they didn't know how to pray.

itswtShuiowwdnkwwotpfbtShifutwg R8.26

IN THE
SAME WAY,
THE SPIRIT
HELPS US
IN OUR
WEAKNESS.
WE DO NOT
KNOW WHAT
WE OUGHT TO
PRAY FOR,
BUT THE
SPIRIT
HIMSELF
INTERCEDES
FOR US
THROUGH
WORDLESS
GROANS.
ROMANS 8:26

COME TO ME,
ALL YOU WHO ARE
WEARY AND BURDENED,
AND I WILL
GIVE YOU REST.
MATTHEW 11:28

ctm
aywawab
aiwgyr m11.28

11

TRUTH When You Need REST

NATALIE

Come to me, all you who are weary and burdened, and I will give
you rest.

—Matthew 11:28

Lay It All Down

My van died this past Sunday.

On the holy day, the day of rest. It was a fitting day to put to rest
the vehicle we brought home babies in, the trusty van we drove
cross-country innumerable times and that never once gave us
a problem—at least not until fourteen years and 120,000 miles
later, when it just died. While my soul mourns just a bit, my children celebrate! They won't have to beg me to wait in the back
of the lot for pickup or skip going to the YMCA for the shame of
rolling up in "that janky van" (true stories). Not that I was mad
about it (though I did sometimes take secret mom joy in embarrassing them with my van). My van was certainly a little worse
for wear, even somewhat embarrassing, but it was *my van*, always
reliable, without any headaches or problems, and I couldn't care

less if someone dinged it or tapped the bumper. It was easy, and I love easy.

But this is hard.

Finding a new vehicle this week has been a lot. My husband is out of town with our eldest for a guys trip (which is fabulous). But we have a million kids with a billion practices, and we need a vehicle . . . *yesterday*! So, while Jason has been a great moral support from far away, most of the burden of searching and calling and driving and deciding has fallen on me. It feels like the entire weight of that new vehicle is sitting squarely on my shoulders right now, and it is crushing me.

So, I haven't been sleeping.

Most of the time sleeping is my secret superpower, my favorite hobby, my dearest friend. But not this week. I'm restless. I toss and turn at night, scrolling the list of SUVs on the back of my eyelids, tallying up our bank balance, wondering whether we should cut back here or there. Sleep comes eventually but doesn't feel restful. I woke up early this morning with the intent of starting on this chapter, but I was so exhausted that I just rolled over to go back to sleep. But instead of finding rest, I just was lying there . . . fretting . . . for an hour. *Ugh.* Finally, I just prayed, "God, please help me with this decision," and I rolled out of bed to start my day.

Thankfully, my work for the day was this verse.

"Come to me, all you who are weary and burdened, and I will give you rest" (Matthew 11:28). *Rest*—the very thing I need right now. *Rest*—what has eluded me these past days. *Rest* for my weary soul. *Rest* for my burdened mind. *Rest* from the crushing weight of getting it right. *Rest* in the arms of Jesus—*real rest.*

Can I tell you this? Just reading that verse made me weep.

The dam broke, and I just poured out my soul to Jesus—all my burdens, all my weariness. I gave him my decision fatigue and my fear of breaking the bank. I gave him my overwhelm from endless scrolling, scrolling, scrolling and my exhaustion from not finding the one perfect thing. I gave him my faithlessness—my lack of trust and my desire to control. Why had I been holding on to all of this as though I could handle it, as if "it's fine, everything is fine," when everything was not fine? Oh, Jesus. He saw. He knew. He heard my plea for help. And he was right there all along saying, "Come to me, give it all to me." And finally, I did, and it changed everything and, well, nothing at all. It didn't change my situation, I've still got a lot ahead of me, and I am not even an inch further in making that decision. *But* everything is different in my soul. The weight of this burden suddenly feels light, like everything doesn't depend on me, not the burden of this vehicle, not our family finances, not any of it. God is the one who carries the weight of our family's well-being; he always has, and he has always been faithful. That's on him, and he is perfectly capable. I can rest in that.

What about you?

Ever feel completely burdened, exhausted, and worn down by life? Ever feel like the weight of all your negative thoughts and worries is just too much for you to bear? Feeling that way right now? Jesus is there calling you to lay it all down. But I want to give you more than my personal testimony. I want to teach you the words of this verse and open up their meaning to you. I want you to understand the breadth of Jesus's offer, so when you speak those words over yourself or to someone else, you know their fullness and beauty and truth. *Yes*, we can lay down our burdens, *yes*, Jesus offers us rest (not just a good night's sleep, but rest for our souls, rest from striving, rest in him). This is the very thing we need. So let's seek out the beauty and the truth in these words, so they can meet us in our need for rest.

The Picture Jesus Paints

Let's read our verse in context so we can see how in just a few short sentences Jesus sums up our problem and his solution.

Come to me, all you who are weary and burdened, and I will give you rest. Take my yoke upon you and learn from me, for I am gentle

and humble in heart, and you will find rest for your souls. For my
yoke is easy and my burden is light.

Matthew 11:28–30

Here's our problem: we are weary and burdened by things that
are too heavy, too big, and simply too much for us. Did you see
his solution? We can come to him and lay down our burdens. In
exchange, he will give our souls genuine rest. But did you notice
what else he gives us besides rest? He gives us something else to
carry. You might think that's strange. Isn't Jesus just exchanging
one burden for another? Well, yes. But don't worry, we'll get there
(and I promise, even that is good news). There are three main
components of this passage I want to look at: our burden, Jesus's
rest, and Jesus's yoke. Let's first discover just exactly what kind
of burden Jesus is asking us to lay down.

Our Burden

In this passage of Scripture, Jesus likens us to beasts of burden,
like oxen or mules. I don't know a lot about beasts of burden,
but strangely enough, I recently cried my eyes out while reading
a story about them. In *Cloud Cuckoo Land* by Anthony Doerr, a
young outcast named Omeir finds his only friendship in his two
beloved bulls, Tree and Moonlight. Life is harsh and unforgiving
for Omeir, but Tree and Moonlight share his burden—they are
his co-laborers, his helpers, even his confidants, and he cares for
them with the tenderness of a mother. But there's a war brewing
in the greater world, and Tree and Moonlight are conscripted to
haul massive components of the war machine off to the distant
battle. And Omeir is forced to drive them, drive them hard like he
never has and never would, drive them for months and months
with little rest, carrying burdens far too heavy for them. Omeir
is helpless to do anything but follow orders and urge his beloved
companions to their eventual death under the heavy, restless
war machine—a machine that cares nothing for him or Tree or

Moonlight. And I cried right alongside Omeir as the burdens overwhelmed and finally broke his companions.

I tell you this story because I want you to catch the symbolism in our passage. Jesus says we are like Tree and Moonlight, weighed down with burdens far too heavy for us, burdens that will overwhelm and eventually break us. We are helpless beasts of burden, weary and worn-out, needing rest but finding none. But unlike poor, powerless Omeir, Jesus isn't helpless; he's powerful and able to save us.

In order to understand the fullness of Jesus's offer, we need to figure out just exactly what kind of burden he's promising to lift from our shoulders. He doesn't say exactly what burdens us and makes us weary, but if we look at the *type* of rest he's offering, we discover the kind of burden he is offering to lift. Notice that Jesus is offering *soul rest* (v. 29). Therefore, the burden he's promising to lift is our *soul burden*. But what can that be? What weighs down our souls? The Bible tells us our sin is what weighs down our souls. When talking about his sin, King David said, "My guilt has overwhelmed me like a burden too heavy to bear" (Psalm 38:4). Our sin is overwhelmingly heavy. And this is our essential problem as humans. We are overwhelmed, burdened, and worn-out by the weight of carrying around our sin.

But what does sin look like, *really*?

In case sin feels like a distant concept to you, or like something some bad guy does in the dark, let me help you see it by showing it to you in me. Sin has a pernicious way of disguising itself in respectability or responsibility or sensibility. Let's look back at my own story. Remember my burden? I was burdened by the weight of doing it all *my*self, *my* way. Here was my sin: I wasn't trusting that God is God and he is in control. Instead, I was trying to control everything—I was striving to do and to be and to achieve . . . *on my own*. My sin wasn't that I failed but that I didn't trust God. Instead, I went my own way,

ctm
aywawab
aiwgyr m11.28

just like our first parents, Adam and Eve, and every person since. This is our human problem: we all think we know best, better than God, so instead of following his way, we go our own way, carrying the burden on our own. But just like Tree and Moonlight, the burden is far too heavy for us and will eventually crush us. The Bible tells us that the result of our sin is disastrous—a curse and our eventual death (Genesis 2:17). When we go our own way instead of following God's way, the burden we carry is the weight of our own sin, and the path we pioneer leads to destruction, not rest.

> **This is our human problem: we all think we know best, better than God, so instead of following his way, we go our own way, carrying the burden on our own.**

Jesus's Rest

What exactly does this soul rest look like? First off, *soul rest*? Yes! Whatever that is, I want that! Rest is the thing we know we need, what we long for. As a means of pointing to our need for his soul rest, God wove rest into the very fabric of our world—creating rhythms of day and night, productivity and restoration, activity and dormancy, wake and sleep. We know deep in our bones that rest is good and necessary. God himself modeled rest from the first. He rested (though he wasn't tired) after his creative work and called his people to do the same each week, saying, "Six days you shall labor, but on the seventh day you shall rest" (Exodus 34:21). More than that, Jesus says, "The Sabbath [day of rest] was made for man, not man for the Sabbath" (Mark 2:27). Did you get that? God made rest *for* us. This is good news to weary people! God made us long for rest so that we might find our ultimate rest, our soul rest, in him.

Soul rest is more than body rest. We've already discovered that our burden is a soul burden, and that burden is our sin. We are worn-out and weary from the effects of sin in the world and in our own hearts. We need more than a spa day or a sleep study to fix our problem. We need our souls to find rest. We need Jesus to lift the burden of our sin and give us his soul rest.

But how does Jesus lift our burden? God in his mercy knew that our soul burden of sin would be far too heavy for us to bear, that it would crush us. So, because of his great love for us, God sent his Son to take our burden and carry it for us. Here's what the Bible tells us about it:

> But he was pierced for our transgressions,
> he was crushed for our iniquities;
> the punishment that brought us peace was on him,
> and by his wounds we are healed.
> We all, like sheep, have gone astray,
> each of us has turned to our own way;
> and the LORD has laid on him
> the iniquity of us all.
>
> Isaiah 53:5–6

Jesus was crushed in our place . . . for *our* sin. The Father took the weight of our sins off our backs and laid them on his perfect Son, Jesus. And Jesus, though being himself God, willingly took off his glory in order to take on our sin and shame. Like a humble beast of burden, Jesus was mortally crushed by the weight of our sin, paying our sin debt with his perfect life. Therefore, the Father raised Jesus not only to life but to glory. So, now Jesus offers life and rest and acceptance to all who would acknowledge their need and give their sin burden to him.

Jesus is calling out to everyone, "Come to me!" This offer of salvation rest is for all who are weary and burdened (i.e., all of us!). Jesus is calling every single worn-out person, anyone who is just so far beyond their own help, so stacked up with sin that it's crushing

TRUTH for Any Trouble

them. Jesus is calling people worn down and exhausted from going their own way, people longing for rest. Jesus says, "Come to me, all you who are weary and burdened, and I will give you rest" (Matthew 11:28). And he says that whoever you are, no matter how far, he will give you what you need—rest for your soul. It's so simple. We just have to come and lay down our burdens and find rest. Why then would anyone *not* come?

But so many don't.

So many doubt it could be true. It makes no sense! But we see it all the time, don't we? Right before our passage, we see just how big of a struggle it is to come to Jesus. John the Baptist sends his followers to make sure that Jesus really is the Messiah—*John the Baptist,* who saw the heavens open and the Spirit of God descend on Jesus, *John the Baptist,* who proclaimed Jesus as the "Lamb of God, who takes away the sin of the world!" (John 1:29). Even John has a moment of doubt and needs one more confirmation. But Jesus doesn't begrudge John his doubt; instead he quotes the prophet Isaiah, pointing out that his miracles confirm that he's the Messiah God promised would come and bring salvation. Jesus says that everyone who believes is blessed. Jesus is patient and constant, confirming his offer to John. And he does the same for any doubter who might need one more reason to believe.

But still many don't believe. In fact, after he confirms his identity, Jesus highlights all the people who don't believe despite his miracles. He lists city after city. Then he explains why, saying, "I praise you, Father, Lord of heaven and earth, because you have hidden these things from the wise and learned, and revealed them to little children" (Matthew 11:25). Jesus says the truth about him has been hidden to some. But here's the surprising part: the people you'd think would see most clearly (the wise and learned) are blind, and the people you'd think wouldn't see much at all (the little children) are the ones who totally get it. The people who think they know aren't humble enough to understand Jesus. But the little children, who are humble, dependent, and needy, they are the ones who see Jesus.

What does all this mean? If we think we're smart enough or strong enough or just "enough" all on our own, if we're convinced we can pull our own weight, or if we're convinced we don't have a burden, then we'll never give it to Jesus. Put simply, if you think you know, you'll never ask Jesus for wisdom. If you think you're self-sufficient, you're not going to ask for help. If you think you don't need Jesus, you might actually need him the most. We don't come to Jesus because we have it all together; we come because we know that we don't.

So, if you don't have it all together, you're in the right place.

I don't know about you, but for me, this is the best news! I don't have to have it all together to come to Jesus. Nope. I simply have to be willing to give him my worn-out weariness. I can lay down my burden right here and now. And so can you. O my weary and burdened friend, this rest is for you! Do you know you need it? That's all you need to know. If you feel the weight of your burden, then Jesus's rest is for you. Whatever it is, you can unburden your soul right now: lay down all the things you carry, all the weight of your striving, all your failures, all of the sin that entangles your feet, all the pressures of perfection, all those negative thoughts that plague you—lay them all down. You don't have to prove yourself anymore. You don't have to carry your own burden anymore. Jesus says to come and give it to him. And in exchange he will give your soul rest, the very thing you need.

O my weary and burdened friend, this rest is for you! Do you know you need it? That's all you need to know.

Wow. That was a lot.

I needed it too. I need this soul rest every day, not just on Sundays! And if this is your first time giving Jesus your burden, you are welcome here. His soul rest is for you, for now and for all time! But here's our ongoing struggle: so often we pick our burden back up, trying again and again to do it by ourselves, going our own way. But even then, even now, there is rest for us. Jesus's compassion and forgiveness and rest never wear out or run dry. His promise is good for today and every day. So I want to encourage you to make this burden-laying-down, rest-finding practice a part of your daily rhythms. I want you to try it for a week. Here's how.

Each day, in the early part of the day, say this verse over your soul: "Come to me, all you who are weary and burdened, and I will give you rest" (Matthew 11:28). Then whatever burdens your soul, give it to Jesus, and ask him to exchange it for his soul rest. Then each night before you sleep do the same thing. And here's the real challenge: during the day when you find that burden back on your shoulders, lay it down again.

Jesus's Yoke

As much as we need soul rest, there's something else we need that Jesus gives us in exchange for our burden: his yoke. I know, this might sound strange. Why do we need another yoke? Didn't we just lay our burden down? I think when you discover just exactly what kind of yoke Jesus gives us you will actually *want* to take it up. Moreover, I'm convinced you'll see that the yoke of Jesus and the rest of Jesus aren't incompatible but actually work together in harmony for our good.

Here's the invitation: just as Jesus invites us into his rest, he also invites us into his work, saying directly after our memory verse, "Take my yoke upon you and learn from me, for I am gentle and humble in heart, and you will find rest for your souls. For my yoke is easy and my burden is light" (Matthew 11:29–30). I know this invitation might not sound as compelling as giving up our heavy burdens and finding rest. But just as our souls need rest, so too do we need activity. If we are weary beasts of burden in need of rest, when we find that rest, we are beasts of burden still—rested, yes, but made for work nonetheless. So Jesus gives us the rest *and* the work we need.

What kind of work are we talking about? The Bible tells us that we were made for work—meaningful, intentional, purposeful work—the kind of blessed work Jesus wants to give us. From day one, God called humanity into his work of extending his fruitful abundance throughout the world (Genesis 1:28). His work isn't the crushing, wearisome burden of going our own way. Rather, it is walking in his good plans *with* him. And here's the cool part: he doesn't need us at all—"He is not served by human hands, as if he needed anything" (Acts 17:25). In our passage, Jesus tells us that the Father has given him all things (Matthew 11:27), yet he doesn't lord his position and power over us. Rather, he is gentle and humble in heart, patiently teaching us his ways and inviting us into life and work with him. He is no harsh master, extracting every last bit of work out of us, as if he really needed our efforts to accomplish his purposes. Rather, he invites us into his purposes for our benefit and for his glory.

Soul work and soul rest are not incompatible.

In the passage we've been studying, we see that soul rest and soul work go hand in hand. But if we look to the passage just after this in Matthew, we see Jesus make this point again. The Pharisees were pitting rest against work, calling the disciples unlawful for picking grain and eating it on the Sabbath (the day of rest). And they were scandalized when Jesus healed a man on the Sabbath. Work and rest were incompatible in their paradigm. But Jesus said to them, "It is lawful to do good on the Sabbath" (Matthew 12:12). Did you catch that? On the actual day that God prescribed rest, Jesus says it is lawful and right to do good. In other words, soul rest and soul work are compatible. Therefore, when we find the salvation rest of Jesus, we also find his salvation work. And what greater work is there than the salvation work of God? These two concepts are

ctm aywawab aiwgyr m11.28

not in conflict but harmonious. When we enter into the salvation rest of God, we also enter into his salvation work. This is the best kind of work, a light burden, an easy yoke.

This is our calling: rest in Jesus and work with Jesus.

Burdens into Rest
By Natalie Abbott

Turn my burdens into rest.
Controlling into trusting,
Earning to receiving,
Scarcity to overflow,
Grasping into giving.
Comparing to encouraging,
All of it now rests on you.

And with your rest, a yoke,
A work that's light and easy.
You who took my burden,
You are burdened still,
Let me be burdened too,
With those that burden you,
Till we all rest together.

My friend, when we experience the freedom from our heavy burdens, when we experience his salvation rest and his loving instruction in our lives, we naturally step into his salvation work. We can't just sit on our hands and not share this message with others! God's original plan for humanity was to multiply and extend his perfect rule in all of creation. And his redeemed plan for us is no different. We are called to join with Jesus in spreading his salvation rest to all people. This is the delight and wonder of God, that he involves us in his beautiful plan to redeem all things. How can this be? What a wonder! What a joy! This is the easy, light, honored yoke of Christ, to be yoked *with him*. To Jesus our Savior be the honor and the glory and the praise for all time! He has invited us into salvation rest *and* salvation work. And it is marvelous! Come and rest. Come and work.

Apply the TRUTH

So what now? What does this look like for you? In your daily life, what would it look like to find this salvation rest?

- What are some of the ways you seek superficial rest when you really need the soul rest of Christ? How can you seek him first for the deep rest you need the next time you find yourself seeking shallow rest somewhere else?

- Maybe there are things you are striving to earn and accomplish and prove, things that you didn't realize you were using to try to earn God's favor. If this is you, you can lay those things down. You can trust that Jesus doesn't need your good works, he just wants your heart. You can rest in him. Write down all the ways you try to carry the burden of your own sin, trying to appease God or pay for your sins with good works.

- Maybe you've always thought you had to earn God's favor, like your good works are what get you into heaven. I hope you've seen that this just isn't the case (thankfully). Jesus bore the burden of your sin for you and earned God's favor with his perfect life. Would you give him your burden and then trust in his rest? If this is you, tell Jesus that you are giving him your soul burdens, and ask him to give you his soul rest instead.

- Maybe you need to remember that God doesn't need your service. He'll get his work done with or without you. But he does want your heart. Maybe there are some things you need to stop doing for a while and just rest in his love for you.

- Maybe there are big, hard things that you need to lay down, things that keep you up at night (those negative thoughts swirling in your mind), things that you haven't trusted God with fully. Oh, friend, God is able and good; give him all of it. He is God—he can handle it. Write out your burdens to God. And when you recognize that you've picked them back up again, lay them down again.

A Prayer for the Weary

Oh, Jesus.

Right now I'm exhausted, completely worn-out. I feel acutely the weight of all the things I'm trying to carry. What rest I get is shallow, fleeting, a temporary escape. Every time I come back to reality, those burdens are still there. I wake up to their heaviness on my chest each morning. I carry them all day long—all my responsibilities, all my people, all the expectations, all the deadlines, the lists, the needs. All these negative thoughts swirl in my head—all the concerns, all the possibilities, all the fretting, all the costs, all the calculating in my mind, all the time. These are all mine, and they are heavy. They overwhelm me. I feel like this isn't how my life is supposed to be. Does it have to be so hard? I long for rest, relief, restoration. Jesus, what do I do?

Rest. Oh, Jesus, you say, "Come and rest. I want you. I know your burden, bring it to me." I want to trust you. I want to believe. Help me where I don't. Help me lay it all down and trust you with every bit of it. Oh please, give me the deep soul rest I need. Help me know you are in control and you will work it all out. Help me give up all my burdens to you.

Amen.

COME TO ME,
ALL YOU WHO ARE
WEARY AND BURDENED,
AND I WILL
GIVE YOU REST.
MATTHEW 11:28

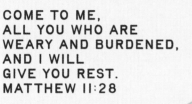

ctm
aywawab
aiwgyr m11.28

I HAVE TOLD YOU THESE THINGS, SO THAT IN ME YOU MAY HAVE PEACE. IN THIS WORLD YOU WILL HAVE TROUBLE. BUT TAKE HEART! I HAVE OVERCOME THE WORLD.
JOHN 16:33

J16.33

IHTYTTSTIMYMHP
ITWYWHTBTHIHOTW

12

TRUTH When You Have TROUBLES

VERA

I have told you these things, so that in me you may have peace. In this world you will have trouble. But take heart! I have overcome the world.

—John 16:33

You *Will* Have Trouble

In this world, I've had my fair share of troubles.

For so many of us, one of the most troubling times in our lives came in 2020. I'm going to share some of my troubles from that season just to help you recall a time when this world seemed to dish out nothing but trouble. If anyone had asked me then, "How are you, *really*?" (that question from chapter 1), I would've most definitely *not* said "good" or "fine." I would have honestly not really known where to start. It was a lot for me, even before the pandemic started.

In early March of 2020, just before the pandemic, my hands were beyond full. I had a newborn and a two-year-old, and our business, Dwell Differently, was really taking off, requiring way more work than I could've imagined. I was sleep deprived, with a two-year-old on my hip and a newborn strapped to my chest, watching my buffer of finished work dwindle away. *How will I do all this? How can I do it well? What will I have to give up? Just how much can I squeeze into twenty-four hours? But really, just how much?* Waves of mom guilt regularly washed over me. And even though there was talk of this thing, the Coronavirus, that may or may not shut down the world, I was unaware. I was in full-blown mom-of-two, business-owner mode. Regardless of the troubles out there in the world, I had enough troubles of my own. Not that my kids and ministry weren't serious blessings! My hands were just really full, and it felt like a lot.

During that same time, Matt came home one day, and he looked like he'd seen a ghost. Something had happened at work that turned my eternally optimistic husband into a shell of himself. All of a sudden my rock, the one who was always lifting me up, needed me to lift him up. Now I added supporting a husband to my toddler, infant, and business. It all felt like a lot. Maybe too much to handle for long.

Then March 11th happened. The whole country shut down . . . officially. I remember the moment when the surgeon general got on TV and told us that this was going to be our generation's Pearl Harbor. *WHAT?! What if this is it for me? What if I get COVID, and I find myself lying in a cold, sterile hospital all alone?* I worried about my grandmother, my parents, my in-laws. *And what about my precious new baby? What would COVID do to a baby?* It seemed there was trouble everywhere I looked. It felt like a lot. Really, really a lot.

For a few months we all treaded water, watching the COVID case numbers and deaths rise. The tension and fear and panic were everywhere. *Do we mask? Do we wipe down our groceries? Do cloth masks work? Should I wear protective glasses too? How can I help? Can I see people? Should I see people? Is that runny nose*

COVID? What if I give someone COVID because I didn't know I had it? My thoughts were a constant negative loop in my mind, and decision fatigue started to set in. It was a lot. Way too much.

Then, in May of 2020, the matriarch of our family, our spirited, colorful grandmother, Abuelita, was coming to the end of her life. All my siblings were going to be with her one last time. I panicked. *What if one of us is sick? What if I contract COVID and expose my new baby? Are we breaking the law to all be in the same car?* If I didn't go, I'd never see my Abuelita again. So, by the grace of God, I chose to go. I got to love and kiss and spend time with my Abuelita one last time before she died. Death. It was the very thing that was constantly lingering in 2020. It was on everyone's mind. And now, we'd lost Abuelita. It was a lot. My heart felt like it couldn't take much more.

During all of this, in late May and through the summer, our country erupted with all the backlash over the unjust killing of George Floyd. And all I could think of was my precious toddler, Isaiah—who had become our son through adoption—a sweet black boy. *How can we, as nonblack parents, raise a black boy?* Though I'd never been disillusioned enough to think that race didn't matter and that love would conquer all our difficulties, thoughts and feelings of inadequacy overwhelmed me. I was afraid of failing at raising Isaiah simply because I'm not black. My soul was wrenched, sick, crushed . . . utterly devastated. In this world I had trouble. And it was all too much. *No more, Lord. Please.*

We All Have Troubles

Not just then, in 2020, but now. All the time. Big and little troubles. In fact, you may be experiencing far greater troubles than what I've just described. Know my heart aches right there with yours.

201

 And even if we are relatively trouble-free, we know it always comes back around. In fact, Jesus says, "In this world you *will* have trouble" (John 16:33, emphasis added). Period. Jesus tells us plainly in our verse that there's no getting around trouble. We have trouble of our own making, trouble from living in a fallen world, and as followers of Jesus, we have trouble from a world that is opposed to him. Any way you slice it, we have trouble and will continue to have trouble.

But let me just tell you what we've already told you in every other chapter in this book—let me just look you in the eye, hold you close, and give you one more promise of God for you in your very present trouble. Jesus has overcome all your troubles. You can take heart! Let's read our verse again. Then we'll look at just how it spoke to the original hearers and how it can speak to us in our troubles: "I have told you these things, so that in me you may have peace. In this world you will have trouble. But take heart! I have overcome the world" (John 16:33).

Trouble, Victory, and Courage!

Trouble

> "In this world you will have trouble."

Jesus had troubles of his own.

With all this talk about trouble, when we look at the context of our verse, we find that Jesus was in the most troubling situation of his earthly life. It's the night of his arrest. The cross is looming, and Jesus knows it. He knows that in the coming hours he will endure betrayal, denial, abandonment, rejection, torture, ridicule, and death. Jesus is facing the most undeserved horror that anyone could imagine. Surely, Jesus has enough troubles of his own, and yet he isn't focused on his own troubles.

Jesus is focused on his disciples' troubles. Trouble for Jesus means trouble for his followers. And Jesus knows every trouble that's coming their way. He tells his disciples that he will soon leave them, which is deeply disturbing to them. But he also tells them that they too will suffer because of him. They will be ostracized from all they've known, kicked out of their communities, and persecuted. People who kill them will genuinely think they're doing God a favor. And in the near term, when Jesus is handed over to be crucified, they will come up short: they will deny him, scatter, and leave him in his own time of trouble. The specific trouble and darkness that the disciples were about to experience was wretched. But the wretchedness of Jesus would be far greater. Yet in that moment, instead of asking his disciples for comfort, Jesus comforts *them*. He calls *them* up into courage, and he promises *them* peace.

The very telling of their troubles is an encouragement. Jesus isn't telling the disciples their future troubles to scare them but to encourage them, though it may not seem like it at first glance. Jesus says, "I have told you these things, so that in me you may have peace. In this world you will have trouble. But take heart! I have overcome the world" (John 16:33). He tells them their upcoming troubles so that they can have peace. As their troubles arise, they can know that Jesus knew. Jesus already told them this would happen. He wasn't caught off guard. Jesus had full knowledge and therefore would have full authority over their troubles, including their ultimate outcome. And just like he tells them their troubles, he also tells them the outcome: victory in him!

Victory

<blockquote>"I have overcome the world."</blockquote>

Did you hear that? "I *have* overcome the world." Lean in right now with me and hear what Jesus is actually saying. We know from what we just learned that Jesus didn't say "I *have* overcome the world" *after* he rose from the dead. He didn't say it from his seat in heaven next to God after the ascension. He didn't say it in glory with angels rejoicing around him. This isn't a victory speech *after* he has already done the thing. No, he says, "I *have* done it" before he actually *has* done it. This isn't what we'd expect at all. We'd expect him to say, "Take heart, I *will* overcome the world" *before* he conquers death, before he's raised from the dead, before Satan's hold on our lives is made powerless. No. Jesus says, "I *have* overcome the world." It's an I-already-did-it statement. Although Jesus is staring down the gauntlet of despair, desertion, and death—and what looks like complete failure to his enemies, to his followers, and to the devil himself—Jesus chooses to say exactly what he says: "I *have* overcome the world."

He declared his victory before he'd overcome anything. Jesus knew and believed that he was victorious despite the circumstances he was facing. Jesus declared his victory in the middle of his trouble. He declared victory not because he thought his circumstances would change. He declared victory not because he thought his friends would always stay by his side and never hurt him. He declared victory not because he thought his enemies would disband and find someone else to torment. No. He declared victory because he trusted his Father to finish what he had promised. He trusted that God the Father would not only accept his sacrifice on the cross but that he would raise him from the dead and seat him at his right hand. Jesus could say "I *have* overcome the world" because he knew it would be so. Period.

> **Jesus declared his victory in the middle of his trouble.**

■ Jesus Overcame His Troubles

We just learned about all the troubles Jesus endured. Did he overcome them? Yes and amen! He did. Every single one of them. Jesus's resurrection from the grave and ascension into heaven were a declaration of victory over every trouble Jesus faced on earth. Where Jesus was rejected and denied, God confirmed his approval. Where Jesus was humbled, he now sat in glory at the Father's right hand. Where Jesus endured death, God granted triumphant life. Surely Jesus overcame all his troubles.

■ Jesus Overcame Our Troubles

Hear me say this. Jesus's troubles were actually all caused by our troubles. Every trouble we have in the world is the result of rebellion against God—Satan's and ours. Some of our troubles are our own fault, some are from other sinners, and some troubles are the result of living in a fallen world. And here's the thing: perfect Jesus, who never made any trouble, willingly endured every single trouble in his earthly life *because* of us and *for* us. He died the death we deserved for our sins. He experienced every scourge, every betrayal, every denial that we deserved. We are the ones causing all of Jesus's troubles, yet he willingly took them all and overcame them all to bring us to himself and to his Father.

■ Jesus Overcame the World

Before we skip along to the courage this brings us, I want to bring up one thing: the world. Our verse tells us that Jesus overcame the world, not just our troubles in it. What does that mean? If you read John 13–18 and circle every time you see the word *world*, you'll get a really good idea. The world doesn't know or believe in Jesus. The world hates Jesus. The world is ruled by Satan and is in opposition to Jesus. Like we just said, the world is full of troubles and troublemakers. But because God so loved this troubled world, he sent his only son, Jesus, into the world, not to condemn it but to save it through him (see John 3:16–17). Jesus didn't come into the world to call down fiery judgment. It was a rescue mission. Jesus didn't overcome the world with righteous condemnation but with his sacrificial love. And right before his greatest display of that love, he told his followers that they were being sent into the world on that same rescue mission. He said it was their love and unity that would show the world who he is and win some out of it. This is how Jesus overcame the world—by rescuing troubled troublemakers out of it and sending them back into the world to do the same.

Courage!

"Take heart!"

Jesus has won the victory! We are overcomers! He has given us his peace, and we are all good, right? It's a wrap. We can head out. But there's this other thing that Jesus says. He says, "But take heart! I have overcome the world" (John 16:33). Why would he tell victors that they need to take heart? Once he dies on that cross and rises again in victory, aren't we all more than conquerors? Why would Jesus say "Take heart!" unless we still would have troubles even after he overcame the world?

We *do* still have trouble.

In this discourse about the world and its hostility, Jesus doesn't promise to rescue his followers from all our troubles. In fact, he prays this: "My prayer is not that you take them out of the world but that you protect them from the evil one" (John 17:15). *Eesh.* Maybe not what we wanted to hear. We are still in it. Jesus intentionally sends us back into the fray, the fray that he himself entered, to rescue other people—people who are right now without hope and without God in the world. This is who we once were. So, Jesus calls us not only to take heart but to have a heart and enter back into the world to call other people out of their troubles and to help them find victory in Jesus.

J16.33

So . . . about those troubles.

We still have them, and they're worth enduring for the good of others. But that doesn't mean they aren't hard. We live in a troubled world full of troublemakers (including us!). And because of that, we will endure hardships of every kind. But here is a balm for our souls: Jesus can relate, and Jesus is with us in them. Jesus, who could've stayed out of it all, entered into our troubles. He understands what it feels like to endure hardship. He knows how it feels to be lonely, rejected, exhausted, grieved, betrayed . . . you name it. So, we can take heart that he's with us in our every trial and trouble. He has not abandoned us to them. He's with us in them, and his Spirit lives in us, comforting, guiding, and giving us peace.

Your troubles aren't forever. We can take heart because we know that Jesus, who overcame the world, is still overcoming it. When Jesus declared, "I have overcome the world," it was before he actually did it, right? It was before he rose from the dead and on to glory. But here's the thing: he's not done yet! Yes, Jesus has overcome. And he is still overcoming the troubles in this world one soul at a time. He has risen, and he now reigns. But he hasn't yet returned. And because he has overcome in every other way, we can trust he will finally overcome our troubles once and for all when he returns to the world one last time. On that day, he will complete his mission of rescue and restoration, making all things new and obliterating our every trouble forever. This is what we were made for—life with him forever without trouble. This is the peace he gives us, not as the world gives, but as only he can. Our hearts can find rest in his promise to return for us.

Apply the TRUTH

- What troubles are you currently facing?
- Now run them through the filter that Jesus has already overcome them. Maybe write them out like this: Jesus

has overcome _____. Even though you don't see the resolution yet, let this encourage your heart that Jesus will overcome them all. Maybe not in the near term, even this lifetime. Still, Jesus is victorious, even over death. And in this, you can take heart.

- Now run them through the filter that Jesus is with you in them. Maybe write them out like this: Jesus is with me in _____. How is it comforting to know he's with you?
- Who is someone in your life who has a lot of troubles right now? How can you pray for them and meet them with the love of Jesus?
- Here's a prayer for when you're troubled:

> *Jesus, you know my pain. You lived here; you were hated, deserted, tormented, used, and left completely abandoned by your friends. Here is the pain I'm feeling: _____. Please meet me in my pain.*
>
> *Jesus, in the face of your own death, you declared victory before it even happened. I want to believe in your victory over the hard things in my life, but that feels impossible. Help me to believe you have victory over: _____. Please bring my heart along to believe you.*
>
> *Jesus, you did overcome this world! You put death itself to death, and one day I will be fully victorious with you. Until then, you promise me peace. Here's where I need peace: _____. Help me have peace even if my circumstances don't change.*
>
> *Jesus, my heart is fearful. I need your courage. Help me believe that you love me and have overcome on my behalf. Here's where I need courage: _____. Help my heart take heart in you, Jesus.*

One reminder: I want to say something important to you. Be gentle and generous with yourself. The practice of taking courage in

Jesus's victory is something you will have to do again and again and again. This world really is full of troubles. It's easy to lose heart. And our enemy, Satan, will remind you daily, moment to moment even, to let your troubles overwhelm you and the darkness consume you. So do this: fold down this page, and when your heart is fretting, come back here and remind your heart to take courage in Jesus.

A Song for Your Troubled Heart

When your troubles weigh down your soul, here is a song to lift you up. It was written by Horatio G. Spafford, who was no stranger to grief. He wrote this song in the wake of the tragic death of his daughters. Speak this song to your heavy heart until your troubles feel lighter, if only for a moment.

It Is Well with My Soul
When peace, like a river, attendeth my way,
When sorrows like sea billows roll;
Whatever my lot, Thou has taught me to say,
It is well, it is well, with my soul.

It is well, with my soul,
It is well, it is well, with my soul.

Though Satan should buffet, though trials should come,
Let this blest assurance control,
That Christ has regarded my helpless estate,
And hath shed His own blood for my soul.

It is well, with my soul,
It is well, it is well, with my soul.

My sin, oh, the bliss of this glorious thought!
My sin, not in part but the whole,
Is nailed to the cross, and I bear it no more,
Praise the Lord, praise the Lord, O my soul!

It is well, with my soul,
It is well, it is well, with my soul.

And, Lord, haste the day when my faith shall be sight,
The clouds be rolled back as a scroll;
The trump shall resound, and the Lord shall descend,
Even so, it is well with my soul.

It is well, with my soul,
It is well, it is well, with my soul.

I HAVE TOLD YOU THESE THINGS, SO THAT IN ME YOU MAY HAVE PEACE.
IN THIS WORLD YOU WILL HAVE TROUBLE. BUT TAKE HEART!
I HAVE OVERCOME THE WORLD.
JOHN 16::33

J16.33

IHTYTTSTIMYMHP
ITWYWHTBTHIHOTW

TRUTH

FOR ALL TIME

13

Keep Singing That Song

NATALIE

My Psalm

They say that smell is our strongest memory-inducing sense. But I wonder if our sense of hearing isn't just as strong. I mean, there are songs that just take us back, aren't there? Every time I hear the song "On My Own" from *Les Miserables*, I am transported back to high school. I remember literally leaning out my bedroom window and belting out that song. I was secretly in love with someone else's boyfriend, and that song gave words to my longing and loneliness. Seems I wasn't very secretive about my feelings though! How overly dramatic and ridiculous! If you know the song, you should be chuckling right now. I am! I'm pretty sure I thought that my Romeo would stroll through our alley, hear my song, and sweep me off my feet. You're welcome for that embarrassing story! But here's the thing: there are places in God's Word that bring me right back to specific times in my life just like that song does.

Let me tell you just a snippet of the words that play like a song on repeat in my life. They come from Psalm 16. Over the course of the past twenty years, that psalm has become my own. Every time

I read that psalm or recite its verses, a flood of memories washes over me—memories of God's specific goodness in different seasons of my life. Those words are my words, the words I have spoken for decades now. When things were lean, I told God that he was "my chosen portion and my cup" (Psalm 16:5 ESV), and I would be satisfied in him. When I needed direction, I said, "I bless the LORD who gives me counsel" and "I have set the LORD always before me" (Psalm 16:7, 8 ESV). When God called us far from home, I told myself, "As for the saints in the land, they are the excellent ones, in whom is all my delight" (Psalm 16:3 ESV). Those words assured me that God would give us a family in his church. In times of barrenness, when it seemed I had no good thing, I said to the Lord, "You are my Lord; I have no good apart from you" (Psalm 16:2 ESV). I can't even write these words, these memories, without tears of gratitude. These are the words of my life, the song I have on repeat in my head.

God's Song

What about you? What's your song on repeat? Do you have places like this in your Bible? Verses that come back at you again and again? God's true words to help you overcome your negative thoughts. My hope for you is that these verses we've learned will become verses like that in your life, and when you read them, you'll be reminded of God's goodness in your life. Maybe you already have some stories of how God has used this time in these verses for good in this season of your life. I'm going to give you the opportunity in a minute to think through the glorious things God has given you in these verses. But before we do that, I want you to see how these verses fit into the big picture of what God is doing not just in your life but in the whole world for all time.

I want you to see the whole song.

I want to take a moment and zoom out and look at those verses you've learned and memorized and prayed through and spoken over yourself! Aren't they amazing? Do you see how they all fit together?

Not just in the beautiful image Vera created of them all together, but in their meaning and substance. They all work together in harmonious unity like verses in God's true, beautiful song. Remember the anthem song of courage that Vera taught you? Remember the verses you learned about God's love and acceptance and guidance and rest? Each one is a different part of the song. Do you hear it now? Is it getting in your head? Is it speaking a better word than the negative thoughts you struggle against? Do you hear God himself singing the words of these verses over you and over all his people for all time? They are the words of his care of you, his presence with you, and his victory for you. They are the words of the numberless multitude in the heavens, singing before the throne and praising God for his "salvation and glory and power" (Revelation 19:1). And we get to sing it with them. They are the best words to the best song.

They'll help you get that annoying *other song* out of your head.

Remember why you picked up this book in the first place? It's because you wanted to get those negative thoughts out of your head—the ones stuck on repeat like a crummy song you wished you could stop singing. Well, the quickest way to get that crummy song out of your head is to sing another better song (to dwell differently, if you will!). This is God's song. And it's what we've labored to teach you (even just a few verses). This is *the* thing: God's Word in your heart and mind overcoming your negative thoughts! This is the song you can keep on singing!

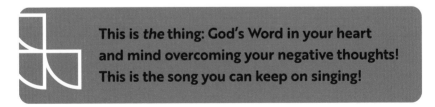

This is *the* thing: God's Word in your heart and mind overcoming your negative thoughts! This is the song you can keep on singing!

Sing God's Song

As we close here I want to take you to one more passage of Scripture that encourages us to sing God's salvation song. Hundreds of years before Jesus came, the prophet Isaiah spoke of a time when the Messiah would come and bring the full salvation of God to his people. Hear what Isaiah tells us about that day:

> With joy you will draw water
> from the wells of salvation.

In that day you will say:

> "Give praise to the LORD, proclaim his name;
> make known among the nations what he has done,
> and proclaim that his name is exalted.
> Sing to the LORD, for he has done glorious things;
> let this be known to all the world.
> Shout aloud and sing for joy, people of Zion,
> for great is the Holy One of Israel among you."
>
> Isaiah 12:3–6

Do you see what God's people do when they come to the wells of his salvation and drink? They are filled up with the joy of their salvation and overflow with singing. And here's the truth: when we come to the wells of God's salvation, we are those people, the ones Isaiah foresaw and prophesied would sing for joy. We are right now living in the day of God's salvation, and Isaiah urges us to *sing*!

So, at the risk of sounding bossy, let me give you some marching orders.

Sing for Joy!

As you go out from here, I hope you *will* "shout aloud and sing for joy" (Isaiah 12:6). I hope that you will "sing to the LORD, for he has done glorious things" (Isaiah 12:5)! I hope you have experienced just a small sliver of the "glorious things" God has promised you in his Word. I hope you have felt his presence and love and care. I hope you have tasted even just a sip of that living water Jesus gives us from the well of his salvation—a well that will never run dry, a well that will fill us with deep satisfaction. When we drink deeply from that well, we overflow with songs of joy.

Sing to the Lord!

Ultimately, the salvation song we sing is *for* God. Isaiah says we are to "Sing *to* the LORD, for he has done glorious things" (Isaiah 12:5, emphasis added). Yes, our song is an expression of our joy, but that expression is ultimately directed at God because of all that he's done for us. We sing *to God* because our joy comes *from* him and was made possible *by* him. Our God has done every glorious thing on our behalf, and our song is our expression of joy and thanks to him—for his lavish love, for his unmerited grace, for satisfying our every need with the free, living water from his well.

> We sing *to God* because our joy comes *from* him and was made possible *by* him.

Sing for All to Hear!

So, our song is a song of joy. It is a song we sing to our God. But there is one more thing we must do. Isaiah says, "Sing to the LORD, for he has done glorious things; let this be known to all the world" (Isaiah 12:5). The final part of this verse is the final piece of Isaiah's puzzle. But for some of us, this is where we screech to a halt and say, "Probably not." If this is you (and it is so often me), hear what Isaiah is telling us. He isn't giving us an evangelism formula. He isn't prodding or guilting us. Not at all. He's simply telling us that when we drink from God's salvation, our response is a song of joy to our God for all to hear. This isn't us trying to muster up courage or the right words to say or strategies here.

We are just people who have joy in our salvation, singing out to God for all to hear. So, if you're like me and struggle sometimes to share your faith, maybe instead of focusing on evangelism, focus on the wonder of your salvation and just see if you don't sing for joy for all to hear!

This Is the Song That Doesn't End

Yes, it goes on and on, my friend! Okay. I'm sorry I just did that to you. But it's true! God's song doesn't ever end; it is the song we will be singing for all eternity. But unlike that ridiculous, mind-numbing kids' song I just planted in your head, God's song doesn't get old or tiresome. It's a song that's always new and beautiful, and there are always new verses to learn. In fact, the more you sing God's song, the more you want to learn other verses of the song. The songwriters of the Bible also felt that way, regularly encouraging God's people to sing a new song, saying things like, "Sing to the LORD a new song, for he has done marvelous things" (Psalm 98:1).

We should always be singing new songs. Now, I hope you have loved learning all the verses we've learned here. I hope you've learned the words by heart and will come back to them often. *But* there are other verses for you to learn. Why? Because our lives are not static, and our songs should not be static either. God is always doing new and marvelous things in our lives, things you will want to sing about. There will be other words that God uses to speak into the new seasons, new challenges, and new situations of your life. There will be other negative thoughts you will need to overcome. Find other words of God to speak into your every need and every joy. And those words will become dear to you. They are words that you can add to the parts of the song you already know. So, keep looking into God's Word and learning more of his glorious song. Sing them for joy, sing them in praise of your God, and sing them to all who have ears to hear about the glory and wonder of our God!

—————— Apply the TRUTH ——————

Okay, so here's the part where you let the words you've learned remind you of the things God has done. I want you to look back at each verse we've discussed, and under each one write one "glorious thing" God did or revealed to you through that verse.

> A good man brings good things out of the good stored up in his heart.
>
> Luke 6:45a

> See what great love the Father has lavished on us, that we should be called children of God! And that is what we are!
>
> 1 John 3:1a

> But blessed is the one who trusts in the LORD, whose confidence is in him.
>
> Jeremiah 17:7

For it is by grace you have been saved, through faith—and this is not from yourselves, it is the gift of God.

Ephesians 2:8

Cast all your anxiety on him because he cares for you.

1 Peter 5:7

Why, my soul, are you downcast? Why so disturbed within me? Put your hope in God, for I will yet praise him, my Savior and my God.

Psalm 42:5

Have I not commanded you? Be strong and courageous. Do not be afraid; do not be discouraged, for the LORD your God will be with you wherever you go.

Joshua 1:9

Show me your ways, LORD, teach me your paths.

Psalm 25:4

In the same way, the Spirit helps us in our weakness. We do not know what we ought to pray for, but the Spirit himself intercedes for us through wordless groans.

Romans 8:26

Come to me, all you who are weary and burdened, and I will give you rest.

Matthew 11:28

I have told you these things, so that in me you may have peace. In this world you will have trouble. But take heart! I have overcome the world.

John 16:33

Vera and Natalie's Personal Takeaways

Every good thing I have is from God.
God loves me and wants me.
God is the only safe place for my confidence.
I can't earn my standing before God.
Jesus is the safe place for my anxious heart.
I can hope in God in the messy middle of my life.
I can be brave because God is with me.
God knows the right path, and he is leading me.
I don't need to have it all together to come to Jesus.
Only Jesus can carry my burdens; they are too much for me.
When I can't pray, the Holy Spirit will intervene for me.
I can find peace in my troubles because Jesus has overcome!

- Which of these verses was the one you needed the most?
- Who could you tell your testimony to of God's goodness to you in your life?
- Did you share any of these verses with someone? How did that go for you?
- What's one situation that you need a verse for right now? Go find that verse! Write it on a notecard. On the other side, write the first letter of every word in the verse and start memorizing it!
- Spend some time praying through these verses, thanking God for the ways he has met you in each specific verse.
- Set the final lock screen image on your phone. It's the one with all the verse images but none of the letters. Let each image prompt you to recall the corresponding verse. If you have trouble remembering a verse, reset it as your lock screen until you remember it. Then set that final image again when you have them all down. Practice reciting your verses every day until they roll off your tongue.

- Want to learn more verses to God's song? We'd love to have you join us at Dwell Differently! Every month we learn a new verse together. Just scan the QR code or go to DwellDifferently.com to become a member.

Our Final Prayer for You

O God,

Thank you for all your good words. They are the good that I have stored up in my heart. Would you bring them to mind when my friends need them? Would you whisper them to me when I need them? Let them become my own words, the words I say in my messy middle, in my dark night. Let them be the good I cling to when things don't look so good. Let them be the truth I say to myself when my feelings are all confused and they don't match up with my head. I will say that you are my one safe place, the sure foundation. Everything doesn't depend on me but on you. And you have given me every glorious thing that I could never earn. You want me and pursue me and love me and call me your own. You will never leave me or forsake me. You are always faithful, even when I am faithless. You never abandon me, even when I abandon you. You always forgive because you are forgiving. And when things get hard, you calm my anxious heart with your care. When the world is scary, I will find my courage and strength in you. When I don't know what to say, I'll trust you to speak for me. When I don't know where to go, you will lead me. Surely, Jesus has overcome all my troubles, and in him, I am yours and you are mine. So I will give you all my burdens in exchange for your rest. Here with you is my peace and my rest, the true joy of my salvation. I will sing your song, now and forever with all the angels and all the saints. All things are from you and through you and for you. To you be the glory and the honor and the praise in my life and for all time.

Amen.

Acknowledgments

VERA

I could list so many people in this space. I often say I feel like God has given me greater than an abundance of people in my life who support me, love me, motivate me, and point me back to Jesus. I'm going to say thanks to some of those folks right here, now. But if ever you've built me up, picked me up when I was low, offered the hug or meal I needed, or pointed me back to Jesus, thank you. I am one of the blessed ones.

To Matt and my boys: When I think of your support, your belief, your sacrifice, and your joy as I've worked on this, I am left speechless. That's why I dedicate this whole thing to you. Matt, you teach me every day about grace, joy, and love. You are my best friend and my teammate. I truly am the most blessed to be your wife. Isaiah, Jordan, and Zion, you boys are my treasure! I wrote this book for anyone who might read it, and I hope one day that anyone is you. To all my boys, I love each of you, and I am forever grateful to God that I belong to you.

To Nat: We did it. It's done. And we are alive! I am so glad you said yes when I asked you to write that first blog. And you haven't stopped saying yes. Rebecca and I always knew you were destined to use that brain for good and God's glory! You are brave, you are talented, and you are called! I can't wait to watch God's plan continue to unfold. Your words reflect the beauty of God's Word, and I am so glad I get to enjoy them! I love you, sister!

To my mom and my dad: You taught me to love art. You gave me a space to play and learn as I grew up, called the creative out of me as I got older, and always led me toward a beautiful finish. Mom, if there was "one last thing" I could do to make it better, you'd help me find it! Thank you! And thank you for instilling in me a love for God. He is the rock. Always.

To Auntie Vera: Thank you for taking me to the Museum of Modern Art in Chicago as a kid. You helped me to love weird and different things. Whenever I would say "I want to be an artist," you always replied with "You *are* an artist." I've always dreamt of doing this kind of work, and you've been my mentor and friend through every step. I could not have done it without you. Thank you, Auntie V.

To my siblings: You each have known me longest, and you love me as little V. My heart swells with joy as I imagine what each of you have taught me about God—all different, all valuable, all beautiful. I am so thankful that you four—John, Rebecca, Natalie, and Curtis—are the ones I can always come back to. So much of who I am begins with you and continues with you. I love you.

To my Abuelita: You were wild and strong, brave and bold. Your courage and tenacity inspire me daily. Whenever I feel like the going is tough, I put on your ring and remind myself of your spirit. I wish you could see the art in this book so you could tell me everything that is wrong with it! *Ha!* Art poured from you with ease, and I am thankful it flowed into my life. I love you, and I miss you every day.

To my Schmitz family: Laurel, about six years ago you told me I'd write a book, and I laughed at you! You knew before I did what God had in store! No surprise there. I always feel supported by each of you—and I feel like I am the luckiest to have each of you. Thank you for always believing in what God has for Matt and me!

To April: Thank you for saying yes. Without your yes, this doesn't exist. Without your yes, I am different, Dwell is different, and fewer people know about the love of Jesus. You teach me every day that I am capable of doing what God calls me to do; I just need to take the next step. Your example leads me every day! Thank you for being our boss! We need you!

To Lisa Jackson, our agent, and the Bethany House team: Thank you for believing in this work before it existed. Lisa, you have humbly led us, been patient with us, and believed in great things for us! It is such a joy to work with you. Thank you for all your help!

To the Dwell team: Kayla, our very first Dwell member, and our very first Dwell team member. You've licked enough envelopes to take us to heaven and back. Sara, you have held up my arms on more than one occasion, always telling me we will make it through! The two of you have been by my side from the beginning, cheering me on, reminding me of who I am and what God is doing, and helping me to see I am never alone. Thank you from the bottom of my heart. Melody, you say yes with bells on. And Lindsay, you point us to truth, always. Without this team, we could never have put this book together. Because of you, God's Word goes out every month, and now it goes out in this book. Your work matters, and I am so grateful for you.

To Ashley, Abbie, and Kayla: You've always been there. You were there in the lowest, darkest moments, which is where Dwell was born. You all have always seen what is in me, and you've helped me have the confidence and courage to get it out! You guys are the best, and I love you. Thank you.

To Lauren and Brian: You teach me love like no one else. Thank you for the privilege of being your friend. I am the lucky one to know each of you. And we will never stop praying.

To Kelsie: When I think of my love for God's Word, I am always taken back to the track, writing verses on my wrist in Sharpie. And

231

when I go there, I think of you. I learned to do hard things with you. God was always our rock in those years of training together. I will ever be grateful for that time with you.

To Carly and Randi: You each were such a big part of my learning to love God's Word. Carly, I always imagined my Bible looking like yours one day, all marked up and underlined. Thank you for showing me what it looks like to love Jesus. And Randi, those early morning coffee dates before school where we'd read together . . . who does that as sixteen-year-old girls? What a gift. I love each of you, and I thank you for being a part of my roots growing down.

To Mer, Madison, and April: Oh, that first time I brought Dwell to you! Just a tattoo to try out—and you guys were in. Thank you for cheering me on in that transition time. I cherish your friendship and each of your hearts to know God more.

And finally, to those first thirty-three members who joined Dwell, to our first followers, and to every one of you since, thank you for letting us be a part of what God is doing in your life. It is a great honor and privilege. May God comfort you, build you up, and be near you now and always.

I love you all,
Vera

NATALIE

I can say ditto to so much of what Vera said, but here are some of my own thanks:

Before I thank all my in-person people, I really want to thank every single Dwell member and follower. This book was inspired by you and is for you. You asked for it. And you've been with us all along—memorizing God's Word with us, sending encouragement and questions, sharing prayer requests and your heart with us. It is my great joy and privilege to get to be a small part of God's work in your lives. You certainly are a big part of God's work in mine. Thank you for joining us on this journey!

To Jason: What can I say to my truest friend? No one is like you. You are iron, sharpening my rough edges and saying the hard things I need to hear. You are a fire, warming my cold feet and lighting the dark times. You are my compass, always pointing my thoughts to True North. And you are my very heart. You have all my love. Thank you for supporting me and loving me well always.

To my kids: You inspire me in so many ways. Josiah, thank you for always keeping me on my toes and asking the hard questions, so many of which I talk about in this book. You are the best conversationalist! Sweet Esti, thank you for being the biggest people lover in the world. I am constantly stretched by your love for others. My Mimi, I am so proud of who you are. Thank you for teaching me strength and kindness and constancy. Ezra, thank you for always bringing the laughs! When things are heavy, you make my heart light. Silas, you are my warm hug. Thank you for the sweetness you bring to our family. You all are such blessings in my life. And this book really is for you. I hope that you learn these verses from God, and I hope they help you know him better and love him more.

To Vera: You are more than a sister. You are my co-laborer in this great, good calling. You are my best coach—you've encouraged me, prayed for me, taught me, laughed with me, cried with me, picked me up and dusted me off, and pressed me to keep on keeping on. You were the first to tell me to write instead of becoming a lunch lady. Thanks for believing God's calling on my life way before I ever did. And thank you for insisting on it.

To Rebecca: My "other" little sister. Thanks for always going first. Thanks for insisting I need to push the cart down the hill when all I want to do is contemplate the grass. Thank you for always pressing me to do the hard thing, *yesterday!* Thank you for late-night talks about life and all the things. You are my confidant *and* my task master. I need both!

To my brothers: Everything Vera said. And thanks for never letting me take myself too seriously. I love you, fools.

To my parents: Ditto to Vera on everything she said. Plus, thanks for letting me walk to the library all by myself after school and all summer long, every summer, even when I was way too young by today's standards.

To Auntie Vera and Abuelita: I echo Vera. Your strength and vivacity have become my own.

To Mike and Julie: You are a testimony in my life of straight-up kindness and generosity and gospel love. Thank you for loving me like your own. Always. Thank you for supporting me and Jason through all the seasons of our lives. You are truly the best.

To Lisa: Thank you for being one of the most quietly awesome people I know. We had *no idea* who you really were or what God had in store when we started picking your brain about a possible book. And then we continued to pester you. *What were we thinking?!* Thank you for your patience and grace with us. Thanks for believing in us. We truly love you.

To Jennifer and the Bethany House team: Thank you for walking through the weeds with us. Thanks (Jennifer especially) for sharing your wisdom with us and patiently holding our hands every step of the way.

To Lindsay: This book is infinitely better because of you. It is far more clearly written, far more theologically sound, and full of content we wouldn't have even thought to put in it. God is so good to give me such a sound sounding board. You are truly a blessing to our ministry and especially to me. Thank you for all your prayers and your friendship.

To Melody: Thanks for picking up all my slack with grace and care. I love you so much. You are not only a true friend, but you are my calendar, my to-do list, and my alert on my phone—all the things I desperately need!

To the Dwell team: Just reread what Vera wrote again. She is spot-on. And I love you all to the moon.

To April: Vera is right. We seriously couldn't have done this without you. Thank you for everything you do (really *every* thing)!

To my 5:00 a.m. baristas: Rory, Z, Jo, and the gang—you guys fill up my cup. Thanks for shining like the sun, especially when it isn't yet!

Notes

Chapter 2 TRUTH to Overcome NEGATIVE THINKING

1. Julie Tseng and Jordan Poppenk, "Brain meta-state transitions demarcate thoughts across task contexts exposing the mental noise of trait neuroticism," *Nature Communications* 11, 3480 (2020), https://doi.org/10.1038/s41467-020-17255-9.

2. Roy F. Baumeister, Ellen Bratslavsky, Kathleen D. Vohs, and Catrin Finkenauer, "Bad Is Stronger Than Good," *Review of General Psychology* 5, no. 4, (2001): 323–370, https://assets.csom.umn.edu/assets/71516.pdf.

3. William C. Bradford, "Reaching the Visual Learner: Teaching Property Through Art," *Social Science Research Network*, September 1, 2011, https://ssrn.com/abstract=587201.

Chapter 3 TRUTH When You Feel UNLOVED

1. Dr. Robert W. Yarbrough, "Lecture 9: The First Epistle of John," YouTube, 55:50, posted by The Master's Seminary, January 16, 2013, https://www.youtube.com/watch?v=VIm7b-noyc8.

Chapter 5 TRUTH When You Feel UNACCEPTED

1. Timothy Keller, *The Reason for God: Belief in an Age of Skepticism* (New York: Dutton, 2008), 71.

2. Tim Keller, "The Centrality of the Gospel," Redeemer City to City, January 1, 2000, https://redeemercitytocity.com/articles-stories/the-centrality-of-the-gospel.

Chapter 6 TRUTH When You're ANXIOUS

1. "Anxiety Disorders—Facts and Statistics," Anxiety and Depression Association of America, October 28, 2022, https://adaa.org/understanding-anxiety/facts-statistics.

Chapter 8 TRUTH When You're AFRAID

1. Kenneth L. Barker, ed., *Zondervan NIV Study Bible*, fully revised ed. (Grand Rapids: Zondervan, 2002), 288.

Chapter 10 TRUTH When You CAN'T PRAY

1. Vera Schmitz, "How to Personally Pray the Lord's Prayer," *Dwell Differently* blog, https://dwelldifferently.com/blogs/bible-memory/how-to-personally-pray-the-lords-prayer.

NATALIE ABBOTT is the cofounder and chief content officer for Dwell Differently, a company that helps people memorize and meditate on God's Word. Natalie cohosts the popular *Dwell Differently* podcast and writes and oversees the weekly blog—teaching the context, content, and application of every verse they memorize. Natalie is a true lover of words. She started following Jesus in college when someone gave her a Bible. She's never put it down and has been memorizing verses ever since.

VERA SCHMITZ is the cofounder and chief creative officer for Dwell Differently. Vera oversees all the design work at Dwell, and she cohosts the *Dwell Differently* podcast along with her sister Natalie. Vera loves seeing God's words come alive artistically in every Dwell design. More than that, she loves seeing people's lives impacted as they memorize them. Vera developed her passion for memorizing God's Word through the rigors of her professional pole vault career. Since retiring from the sport, she's learned that having a strong mind grounded in God's truth is even more important for "real life" than for athletics.

Learn more at DwellDifferently.com